ASPECTS OF JEWISH ECONOMIC HISTORY

ASPECTS OF JEWISH ECONOMIC HISTORY

MARCUS ARKIN

THE JEWISH PUBLICATION SOCIETY OF AMERICA

Philadelphia

ACKNOWLEDGMENTS

I should like to thank the editors and publishers
of the following journals and newspapers for permission
to use material that initially appeared there:
Historia Judaica (New York)
Jewish Affairs (Johannesburg)
The Jewish Digest (Houston)
New Nation (Pretoria)
South African Jewish Chronicle (Cape Town)
South African Journal of Economics
South African Zionist Record (Johannesburg)
Temple Brotherhood Annual (Port Elizabeth)

TO SUE

CONTENTS

ILLUSTRATIONS

PREFACE

As an economic historian by training and inclination, I have found myself increasingly drawn toward the Jewish aspects of the economic development of the Western world. For far too long Jewish economic history has been viewed as an appendage of the historical model-builders, ranging in infinite gradations from the "fossil of history" views of the Toynbee school to the dominant role suggested by the Sombartians; but in vain have I waited for an abler pen than mine to take an objective stance within the broad sweep of socioeconomic history.

No attempt is made here to provide a comprehensive survey of Jewish economic history. The topics are simply those which have happened to interest me in a series of busman's holidays away from more esoteric research projects. Many of the pieces were originally review articles or essays written for some special occasion. Some of them contained a good deal of footnote material, most of which has now been deleted for fear of upsetting that mythical creature "the general reader," for whom this collection is intended; those anxious to probe deeper will find appended an annotated select reading list. The astute reader will notice a few cases of material overlapping where trends are viewed from different perspectives—but I hope he will not also detect too many contradictions.

These pieces do not claim to draw any lessons from history, but I am acutely aware of the fact that the relationship between the Jews and the "dismal science" is a difficult one if only because of that age-old problem, "Who is a Jew?" For example, consider the career of Sir Ernest Oppenheimer (d. 1957), founder of the giant Anglo-American Corporation, who came from an Orthodox German Jewish family. There can be no questioning the fact that Oppenheimer's initial successes in the diamond industry were owing to his close ties with Jewish firms like Dunkelsbuhler & Co. (whose agent he was on first arriving in South Africa) and the Rothschild organization—firms which in the early years of this century dominated the international gem trade. Oppenheimer's Jewish connections were an integral part of the circumstances that accounted for his rise to tycoon status in the mining world.

Yet in a detailed study of Sir Ernest's business career, which runs to well over six hundred pages (*Ernest Oppenheimer and the Economic Development of Southern Africa* [Oxford, 1962]), Sir Theodore Gregory, himself one of the most eminent writers on monetary economics British Jewry has yet produced, makes no mention of this essential Jewish background—a major analytical flaw in an otherwise admirable study.

I mention this as an extreme instance of the tremendous difficulties confronting any assessment of the Jewish contribution to economic progress. Within the past few decades a number of important monographs have appeared, based on original manuscript sources, which are specifically devoted to particular aspects (some of them very narrow indeed) of this vast and formidable subject. These will make it possible to treat great parts of the field anew and in a much more scientific manner.

In the interim I hope that the present work may serve to cut some narrow channel that will link the rising lake of specialist probings with the broad ocean of Jewish historical research, which generally has disregarded economic trends, enabling the waters of each to flow more easily into the other.

M. A.

I

ANTIQUITY

1

FARMING
IN BIBLICAL TIMES

The Bible means different things to different readers; it has been the source of more argument and friction, of more discussion and reinterpretation than any other text ever published. Today it still has the power of provoking a multitude of reactions, which range all the way from word-for-word literal acceptance to cynicism and absolute disbelief.

Archeologists, anthropologists, and other types of investigators concerned with various aspects of society in the ancient world usually find themselves, at some stage of their research, trying to substantiate or refute a particular thesis by referring to specific biblical passages; and the worldwide interest in the Dead Sea Scrolls is merely another symptom of the continuing importance of biblical studies in scientific research. Anyone genuinely interested in the history of antiquity—irrespective of his views on religion—cannot afford to ignore the most valuable source book on the evolution of society and its institutions in the ancient Near East.

Of all these scholars, perhaps it is the economic historian who is the most fortunate: the data with which he is primarily concerned, by their very nature, are much less subject to controversy or ambiguity. This is especially so with the most basic of all economic activities—agriculture. Scattered about in the Hebrew Bible are continual references (some of them extraordinarily clear and detailed) to agrarian matters. These allusions not only throw a good deal of light on farming arrangements and rural conditions, but also suggest that the techniques of husbandry were somewhat more complex than is generally imagined and that some of the social problems flowing from the organization of agriculture which were to confront many later communities were not unknown to the Hebrews.

The ancient Israelites first emerge from the dim mists of a legendary past as a nomadic pastoral people; in fact, the association of Cain with land cultivation, while his brother, Abel, was "a keeper of sheep" (Gen. 4:2), clearly implies disparagement of tilling the soil. Abraham is represented as a nomad par excellence, and it is only after the conquest of Canaan that the Hebrews begin to become sedentary, crop-growing farmers. Even then, in some districts not well suited to constant tillage the principal means of subsistence continued to be the rearing of sheep and goats, involving a limited nomadism because of the seasonal alternations of pasturages. This was the case in the south of Judah (see, for example, 1 Sam. 25) and among the tribes of the trans-Jordanic plateau (Judg. 5:16), which in the days of Ahab paid a tribute of 100,000 lambs and the wool of as many rams (2 Kings 3:4). Yet tillage rather than a pastoral life had become prevalent after the settlement in Canaan, and the tendency was for the peasant to sell his goats and purchase a field with the profits of the transaction (Prov. 27:26).

A wide variety of crops came to be cultivated, the most important always being wheat. In good seasons, when the harvests exceeded local demands, considerable quantities were exported, especially to Israel's northern neighbors, the

Phoenicians (Ezekiel refers to the practice in his lamentation for Tyre [27:17]). Barley was the second major crop and apparently formed the staple food of the poorer classes (see Ruth 3:17); other food crops included millet, beans, and lentils. At least one plant was cultivated for manufacturing purposes—flax, for linen and sailmaking (the hackling process is alluded to in Isa. 19:9).

Of great importance was the culture of the vine and the olive, and figs were also cultivated extensively. To "dwell safely, every man under his vine and under his fig-tree" (1 Kings 5:5) became the goal of every Hebrew husbandman. Viticulture demanded more attention and labor than the others, since the stony slopes, whose thin layer of topsoil was easily washed away by the winter rains, had to be carefully terraced (Isa. 5:2). Both "grape-blood" (Deut. 32:14) and olive oil became valuable export items, and Solomon paid at least part of his debts to Hiram in oil (1 Kings 5:25).

By the time of Saul and David the method of tillage had advanced from hoeing to plowing. The ox-drawn plow used by the Hebrews was a light, simple affair, and its modern counterpart is still to be found in many districts of Syria and the Nile Valley. It consisted of wooden beams and supports, but the wearing parts were fashioned from iron (as is clearly indicated by Isaiah's famous prophecy that "they shall beat their swords into plowshares" [2:4]). The sowing season was seldom a joyful one, apparently, owing to the vagaries of the Palestinian weather and the heavy expenditure of energy on the hard, rocky soils; the author of Ecclesiastes urges the constant attention of the husbandman to the young seedlings (11:6), Isaiah advocates placing the seeds into furrowed rows instead of scattering them broadcast out of a basket (28:25), and Joel refers to new seeds shriveling under the clods in a season of severe drought (1:17).

In the interim between sowing and reaping the crops were

constantly exposed to a host of natural hazards: hailstorms were not unknown during the months of March and April (Hag. 2:17); weeds were a problem (Jer. 12:13); crops were subject to a whole catalog of fungus diseases, among them mildew (Deut. 28:22); and of course farmers were plagued by the ravages of the locust, mentioned in many contexts. The grape grower had to be especially wary of "the little foxes" (Song 2:15) and of the wild pig (Ps. 80:13), but all the crops were in danger from the inroads of cattle. Clear provision is made (Exod. 22:4) for the payment of compensation if beasts have pastured in a neighbor's unharvested field.

The commencement of harvesting operations varied according to elevation, exposure, and local fertility: in the neighborhood of Jericho the cereal harvest started around the middle of April, on the coastal plains about ten days later, and in the high-lying areas as much as a month afterward; the work would continue for about forty days (Deut. 16:9).

The sickle used for cutting the grain is never described in any detail by the biblical authors, but apparently two types were employed (see Deut. 16:9 and Jer. 50:16), the more popular variant being a wooden implement toothed with flints and believed by Prof. W. M. F. Petrie to have been designed to resemble the jawbone of an ox. Since the weather during these harvest weeks was usually rainless, threshing would take place in the fields themselves. When only small quantities of grain were to be handled, threshing was a simple operation with hand flails (Ruth 2:17); where large amounts were involved, a sledge of large weighted boards, with sharp stone chips attached to the underside and drawn by a team of four or five oxen, would shell out the grain from the sheaves spread out over the floor (2 Sam. 24:22; Job 41:22).

When the threshing was finished, winnowing began; the

grain was separated from the chaff by means of a special wooden fork (Jer. 15:7), with the evening wind scattering the chaff (Ps. 1:4); the straw left over after threshing served as a valuable cattle fodder (Isa. 65:25). The grain would then be collected into large heaps, and until it could be safely stored the farmer might have to sleep on the threshing floor to prevent theft, as Boaz did (Ruth 3:7); in addition, underground silos were known to the biblical Hebrews (Jer. 41:8).

The joy of harvesttime in ancient Israel was proverbial (Ps. 126:6), the festivities culminating in Shavuoth (the Feast of Pentecost), a nature festival that specifically celebrated the ingathering of the wheat (Exod. 34:22) and was gradually incorporated into the cycle of religious holidays. Succoth (the Feast of Tabernacles) celebrated especially the harvest from olive groves and vineyards, as well as the close of the husbandman's labors as a whole (Deut. 16:13).

Although there is little specific biblical information on yields and returns, the general impression is that until the monarchial schism in the late tenth century B.C.E. the majority of yeomen-farmers had little difficulty in making ends meet. Thereafter, however, the writings of the prophets indicate a steady process of social differentiation. As often happens in a predominantly self-sufficient community of smallholders when tribal cohesion and kinship loyalties become weaker in the face of more effective central government, some farmers grew richer at the expense of their fellows and various forms of exploitation appeared. The Book of Amos, for instance, harps on the various burdens of the small farmers (public taxes, private usury, and so on), and stresses that many of them were hardly making a livelihood. The accumulated fruits of years of labor could easily be destroyed by the havoc of foreign invasion, alternating drought and floods, or locust plagues, and each such catastrophe would tend to weaken the position of the less able or less thrifty peasant and strengthen the hand of a neighbor with more skill or initiative. In fact, the situation was not basically different from what was to take place among the people of Latium in central Italy four centuries later: many farmers eventually lost their holdings altogether, and a small group of comparatively rich landowners began accumulating large estates.

Isaiah's passionate exclamation, "Ah,/Those who extend house up to house,/And join field to field,/Till there is room for none but you/To dwell in the land!" (5:8; see also Mic. 2:1–2), clearly indicates that intellectual leaders were fully aware of the trend's inherent dangers. Moreover, the tale of King Ahab and Naboth (1 Kings 21) shows how pseudolegal forms of expropriation were being employed by powerful landholders; the same tale demonstrates the psychological effects of such threats—Naboth persistently refused to surrender his inheritance out of fear of being reduced to the status of a landless man, which in Israel (as in ancient Babylonia and Egypt) was a far from enviable position.

Those poorer peasants who tried to stave off the inevitable by borrowing from wealthier neighbors frequently ended up by being even worse off. Since the agricultural output of most holdings would not bear the strain of prevailing high interest rates, they would be permanently ruined by such debts. The frequent warnings against suretyship found in the Book of Proverbs (for example, 6:1, 11:15, 20:16) indicate severe treatment of defaulting debtors, while an incident concerning a deceased husband who had incurred a moderate debt (2 Kings 4) clearly reveals that the creditor had the right to exact payment from his widow in the form of labor services. This tendency must have been aggravated in the ninth century B.C.E., when the Syrian wars desolated the borders, and those smallholders who had lost their crops through the ravages of the invader (see Jer. 6:12) were driven to borrow at

Gezer Calendar showing yearly cycle of agricultural seasons; thought to be earliest Hebrew inscription (10th century B. C. E.?)

rates as high as 25 percent. Consequently, many impoverished debtors became the bonded servants of more prosperous farmers, at least for a time, and when the term of servitude was over, the only course open to them was to join the swelling ranks of landless workers and hire themselves out on the large estates.

Although there are some biblical references to annual and triennial employment contracts (for example, Isa. 16:13, 21:16), the majority of these wage earners appear to have been hired on a day-to-day basis with little security of tenure, so that seasonal unemployment must have been considerable. Furthermore, with growing urbanization and the establishment of permanent royal courts, many of the bigger landowners were induced to live all year around in Samaria or Jerusalem, leaving the administration of their estates to professional farm managers; the upshot of such absenteeism was agricultural mismanagement and an increase in localized rural oppression.

It is not surprising, therefore, that this miserable state of a considerable segment of the peasantry should have aroused both the pity and the indignation of the eighth-century B.C.E. prophets, who rebuked the avarice of the wealthy landowners and upbraided those harsh creditors who sold their victims into virtual slavery (for example, Amos 2:6, 8:6). This prophetic campaign was not without positive results and was to culminate in a system of laws designed to protect and alleviate the rural indigent.

A whole series of statutory regulations relating to the harvested crops and noteworthy for their humanitarianism had first appeared in the Book of Deuteronomy: a tenth part of the yield of every third year was to be kept for the use of the poor (14:28); the wayfarer was entitled to pluck sufficient from the standing grain to satisfy his hunger (23:25); and any sheaf forgotten in the field was not to be retrieved but left "for the stranger, the fatherless, and the widow" (24:19).

This strongly marked humane tendency so characteristic of Deuteronomy was reinforced and carried very much further in the late priestly code. For example, the old custom of leaving the margins and corners of each field unreaped so that the hungry could benefit thereby eventually became an express grant to the poor (Lev. 19:9). The climax in this movement was reached with the enhancement of the sabbatical year (to insure a fallow season for the land every seventh year) into a year of jubilee, which provided that every fiftieth year all property pledged because of poverty was to be restored and that anyone who had been forced into servitude on account of debt was to be set at liberty (Lev. 25:25–28, 39–41). There can be little doubt that these two main elements of the jubilee—personal emancipation and the return of mortgaged property to its hereditary owner— were intended to abolish rural poverty and to overcome the problem of a landless peasantry.

Of course, it was impossible to enforce such a utopian enactment properly; the earlier Deuteronomic legislators had displayed soberer judgment by asserting that "there will never cease to be needy ones in your land" (15:11). Nonetheless, here were the first timid gropings toward tackling a problem that has perplexed mankind down the centuries and into the era of the welfare state.

2

TRADE AND INDUSTRY
IN BIBLICAL TIMES

While agriculture was the overruling force shaping the Hebrew economy during the biblical epoch, the ancient Israelites were by no means concerned exclusively with self-sufficient farming activities. The regular exportation of surplus crops, a pronounced urbanization movement (in Israel and Judah, an area covering less than eight thousand square miles, there were no fewer than four hundred settlements classifiable as towns), and, in the later period of the monarchies, the growth of large estates and the appearance of a landless peasantry all suggest that trading and industrial pursuits were not wholly insignificant. In fact, a scrutiny of the biblical text serves to cast serious doubts on the oft-repeated assertion that the Jews were not originally a commercial people and that it was only after the dispersion that they were commercialized by force of circumstances.

Owing to its strategic location on the main trade routes, Palestine had an importance in antiquity that was quite disproportionate to its size and natural resources. The normal flow of traffic between the valleys of the Euphrates and the Nile crossed the land of Israel from northeast to southwest, while from south to north the country was traversed by the caravan road that linked Arabia with the great commercial cities of the Phoenicians. A caravan, according to William Cunningham, "not only serves to convey goods great distances, it is also a moving market or fair which is opened at successive stages" (*Western Civilization in Its Economic Aspects* [Cambridge, 1923]); people living along such routes gain certain advantages from the transit cargoes—they can supply the merchants with provisions, they are able to purchase foreign luxury articles, and they have the opportunity to serve as brokers and intermediaries. Numerous allusions in the Hebrew Bible suggest that as a result of such a favorable geographical location there was a wide diffusion of "commercial spirit" among the Israelites and that, contrary to popular opinion, they were in advance of many neighboring communities in this respect.

The potential economic benefits flowing from this situation were modified, however, by the fact that for many centuries a narrow belt of foreign territory separated the Hebrew people from the Mediterranean coast. The ports to the north of Carmel were in Phoenician hands, and it was not until 144 B.C.E. that the harbor of Joppa (Jaffa) passed into the possession of Israel (in fact, this very poor roadstead is never mentioned by the preexilic chroniclers). Throughout the Hebrew Bible the sea is portrayed as a power hostile to God and man (for example, Ps. 93; Job 7:12; Isa. 17:12ff.), and it is extremely doubtful that the Israelites ever operated trading vessels on the Mediterranean before the Persian era.

Mercantile caravans passing between Egypt and Mesopotamia and crossing the Plain of Jezreel to and from the desert southlands must have been a familiar sight to the nomadic Hebrew wanderers, even in the early days when Joseph was sold as a slave by his brothers, and there are indications in Genesis (37:25, 43:11) that these clans sometimes carried goods between Syria and Goshen or escorted cargoes passing through the district which they occupied.

For some time after the permanent settlement in Palestine much of the transit trade remained in the hands of the original inhabitants, and the term "Canaanite" became a synonym for merchant (Job 40:30; Prov. 31:24); from them the Israelites would procure foreign goods, partly by barter, partly through plunder (one such example is the episode of Achan's mantle from Shinar, Josh. 7:18–21), while they occupied themselves with herding and cultivation. The gradual unification of the tribes promoted regional interchange (such as the livestock products of the pastures for the wheat of the grainlands), and the growth of townships encouraged commercial farming. With the establishment of the monarchy, direct Israelite participation in external commerce gained in significance.

There are numerous scattered allusions to this trade, but the leading instances are the accounts of Solomon's mercantile activities in the First Book of Kings; what is found there applied, in varying degrees, to the whole period of the monarchy. Solomon's interest in foreign commerce stemmed from a number of circumstances: close ties with the Phoenicians had made him fully aware of its likely benefits; his successful conquests had brought into the country considerable quantities of hitherto unfamiliar goods as gifts or tributes (5:3, 10:10, 25). At the same time, an increasing supply of foreign articles was needed to meet the luxury demands of the royal court, to support his elaborate program of building expansion in Jerusalem, and to equip the armed forces.

Through David's conquest of the Edomites, the Hebrews had gained direct access to the sea. Thus, in alliance with Hiram of Tyre, who supplied timber, shipbuilders, and skilled Phoenician mariners, "king Solomon made a navy of ships at Ezion-geber, which is beside Eloth, on the shore of the Red Sea, in the land of Edom" (9:26). Thereafter this fleet sailed every three years to the mysterious land of Ophir, which Prof. W. F. Albright suggests was located on the East African coast in the neighborhood of modern Somaliland. Ophir, apparently, was something of an entrepôt for the early commerce of the Indian Ocean, and the squadron would return with treasure and a miscellaneous collection of exotic items: "gold and silver, ivory and apes, and peacocks" (10:22). The land traffic, which came to be organized as a government department, included extensive imports of wood from the Lebanon ranges (5:20), linen, chariots, and horses from Egypt—some of the war steeds being resold to the Hittites (10:28–29).

Such imports implied corresponding exports: Solomon contracted to pay for the labor and materials furnished by Tyre in olive oil and wheat (5:25); in other connections we read of spices, balm, myrrh, honey, and almonds going to Egypt; other local exports may be inferred from the existence of fertile vineyards and inland fisheries. Yet an allusion in a corrupt passage of the text (10:15) seems to suggest that heavy tariffs were imposed on the transit traffic between Arabia and the Levant in order to help balance the great disparity between the value of imports and exports during Solomon's reign.

The political and civil disturbances after Solomon's death must have put an end to the Red Sea trade, since the only other reference to commerce between Ezion-geber and Ophir is the statement (22:49) that Jehoshaphat made a fruitless attempt to renew it. But this disappearance of the ocean outlet may have been offset by an upswing in the northern land traffic, for we learn that Ahab, after his victory over Ben-hadad and the Syrians, secured the right to establish Israelite trading quarters in the markets of Damascus (20:34).

The observations of the eighth-century B.C.E. prophets on

the material prosperity and love of luxury in the two kingdoms (see, for example, Isa. 2:6–7; Hos. 2:10, 10:1; Amos
6:3–6) imply a sustained demand for foreign goods. The
subsequent expansion of Assyrian power and the eclipse of
Samaria must have resulted in a serious shrinkage of external
trade.

Since the land of the Bible was well supplied with the
products of the most advanced industrial civilizations of the
time, its situation at the crossroads of far-flung commerce
proved something of a hindrance to the development of local
manufacturing industry. Nonetheless, Cunningham's assertion that "at the time of their greatest prosperity, the people
of Israel had apparently made no progress in industrial skill"
(op. cit.) is much too sweeping.

Although the products of Egypt, Chaldea, and Phoenicia
were all readily available, the grave risks and high costs entailed in transport in the ancient world made them relatively
expensive, so that their consumption would have been
confined to the wealthier segments of the urban population.
In the smaller towns and villages female domestic labor took
care of most family needs: spinning and weaving garments
were regular tasks for the housewife (1 Sam. 2:19), who also
fashioned finer linen fabrics for sale to itinerant merchants
(Prov. 31:24), although the priestly code forbade the inter-
weaving of linen and wool (Lev. 19:19). The mention of a
field outside Jerusalem named for the fullers (2 Kings 18:17)
suggests that some of the coarse cloths woven in the peasant
cottages were taken to urban specialists to be cleaned and
finished off. The art of dyeing is not mentioned in the Scriptures, but colored stuffs are referred to in numerous passages
(for example, Exod. 26:36; Prov. 31:22), so it is probable that
the technique was known to the Israelites.

The art of the potter, too, was undoubtedly widespread in

biblical Israel, and is a favorite source of prophetical meta-phor (for example, Isa. 29:16, 45:9). There were settlements of potters in the lower city of Jerusalem, where Jeremiah found them shaping their clay, working their wheels, and attending their furnaces (Jer. 18:2–4). Yet recent excavations show that Hebrew potters mainly imitated foreign models in a somewhat crude fashion; except for price, the native prod-uct could not easily have competed with the wares imported by the Phoenicians from Cyprus and Crete from the ninth century on.

The extensive building operations of the monarchial pe-riod made masonry a major industry, and the measuring line, the plumb line, and the mason's level became familiar terms (Isa. 28:17; Amos 7:7; 2 Kings 21:13). The detailed accounts of architectural activities in Jerusalem under Solomon (1 Kings 6:1ff.), however, make it clear that in the construction of the Temple, the erection of city walls and fortifications, and the building of reservoirs, the Hebrews were heavily dependent on foreign skills and materials—especially those of the Phoenicians.

Yet the people of the Book did attain eminence in at least one industrial occupation: metalworking. During the tribal era Hebrew smiths had fashioned weapons and a variety of implements (Deut. 19:5, 27:5), and the wily Philistines con-sidered it prudent to deport all smelters, "lest the Hebrews make them[selves] swords or spears" (1 Sam. 13:19). Subse-quently, David's victories in the north, which brought in an abundance of iron ore (2 Sam. 8:8), the development of the Phoenician tin trade, and Solomon's exploitation of the Ne-gev's copper deposits (evidence for which was provided by the 1937 Glueck excavations) ushered in a brilliant period of metallurgy, and the Temple was embellished with adorn-ments fashioned from molten bronze (1 Kings 7:13ff.). The aptitude which the Jewish people have displayed through the centuries in the working of the precious metals also found a ready outlet in Solomon's love of costly splendor: "And all King Solomon's drinking-vessels were of gold, and all the vessels of the house of the forest of Lebanon were of pure gold" (1 Kings 10:21). In addition, he ordered two hundred large shields to be set up, each containing three hundred pounds of beaten gold, while his great throne was overlaid with gold foil (1 Kings 10:16–18). With orders of such magnitude, the art of the goldsmith must have made tremendous progress, but even at a much earlier time fine priestly garments were being woven from golden threads (Exod. 39:3).

The fact that only a small number of separate crafts are mentioned in biblical literature would suggest that division of labor was not very pronounced; moreover, there was only one word, *harash* (literally, "hewer"), to designate three different kinds of workman: woodman, cabinetmaker, and stonecutter. In the cities craft specialization was more pronounced, and there was also a certain amount of occupational segregation; in Jerusalem, for instance, bread was supplied by professional bakers who lived in a special street (Jer. 37:21), where separate groups of locksmiths and barbers were also to be found. Although a guild of potters is mentioned by the chronicler (1 Chron. 4:23), it was only after the Babylonian exile—and probably as a result of industrial experience gained during the years of captivity—that the grouping of artisans in Jerusalem into such craft associations became general (Neh. 3:31). Since particular occupations were originally a clan affair (Gen. 4:20), it seems reasonable to assume that trades were also hereditary in certain families.

All in all, industry appears to have played a somewhat more important part in the economic life of the Israelites than most historians are prepared to acknowledge.

*   *   *

Scattered biblical references give some slight indication of how business practice kept pace with the development of commerce and manufacturing. There is evidence that by the eighth century B.C.E. a combination of barter and the use of money in transactions was widespread (Hos. 3:2), while even in nomadic times silver shekels had been a frequent unit of payment (for example, Gen. 23:15; Exod. 21:32). But throughout the whole period ending with the fall of Jerusalem and the Babylonian exile no *coined* money was employed, and for every transaction all ingots had to be carefully weighed (Gen. 23:16). Since trading dishonesty is always a problem in an age of sporadic marketing contacts, from the time of the earliest prophetic writings on there were repeated warnings against the use of unjust weights (Prov. 11:1; Mic. 6:10ff.; Amos 8:5) and strict injunctions against falsifying the balance (Deut. 25:13–16; Lev. 19:35–36).

Since the early days of settlement in the land of Canaan the priestly shrines had served as banks to the extent of receiving money and other valuables for safe deposit (Judg. 9:4), but in the Hebrew Bible there is absolutely no trace of embryo bankers to provide finance capital or credit facilities.

Yet one sign of "capitalistic" progress is furnished by the rules regulating interest. Originally interest payments on money loans were strictly forbidden (Exod. 22:25), since lending was regarded as a purely benevolent action and there was no notion of funds being borrowed for business purposes. Subsequently, as the Israelites gradually became involved in the transit commerce with Egypt, Arabia, Phoenicia, and the East, charging interest was permitted in the case of a foreigner (Deut. 23:21), although this modification is mentioned with disapproval by a later psalmist (Ps. 15:5).

A further provision in the Deuteronomic code (15:1ff.) regarding the canceling of debts in the "year of release" refers to charitable loans only, not to advances for business purposes. The emphasis both in the Mosaic code and in the writings of the later prophets is on protecting the debtor against unjust treatment, and there appears to be no biblical stipulation for the recovery of a loan—although the non-repayment of a debt is condemned (Ps. 37:21). As has been previously indicated, however, there is little doubt that toward the end of the monarchial period the large estate owners were able to lend money during bad times at exorbitant rates on the security of the borrowers' lands, which were forfeited when the repayment obligations were not discharged.

There is direct mention in the Hebrew Bible of only two or three other elementary points of business ethics, such as the duty of fair dealing (Deut. 24:15), the danger of greed (Jer. 8:10; Mic. 2:2), and the extension of hospitality to the commercial traveler (Deut. 10:19).

One broad generalization that emerges from this brief survey is that in the main the ethicoreligious ideals which chiefly concerned the biblical philosophers and lawgivers are not in direct conflict with the concept of economic progress. If the Book of books displays a relative indifference toward earthly riches, it nevertheless encourages hard work, exalts individual freedom, and looks upon genuine enterprise as a virtue. Composed in a society that was disturbed more than most by spiritual matters, the Hebrew Bible reveals a lively awareness of economic affairs.

Nor are these biblical references of merely antiquarian interest: in the modern state of Israel questions of cultivation, afforestation, mineral prospecting, and industrial planning are frequently decided on the basis of exact historical information provided by a literary monument that dates back more than three thousand years. If and when the Israelites of the twentieth century surmount their economic difficulties, their success in no small measure will be due to the continuing influence of the Bible: "I will cause the cities to be inhabited, and the waste places shall be builded. And the land that was desolate shall be tilled, whereas it was a desolation in the sight of all that passed by. And they shall say: This land that was desolate is become like the garden of Eden" (Ezek. 36:33–35).

3

AN ECONOMIC SURVEY
OF JEWISH LIFE
DURING THE PAX ROMANA

The Roman Imperial Peace, the Pax Romana, which extended from the time of Augustus Caesar down almost to the close of the second century of the Christian Era, was a golden age of economic advancement for the peoples of the ancient world. While it lasted the entire Mediterranean basin, a considerable portion of the Middle East, and much of Europe north of the Alps were welded together into a single prosperous unit, and, under conditions of stable government, effective land and sea communications, and a uniform currency, an unprecedented movement of goods and services, of craftsmen and techniques took place.

One of the regions that did not enjoy the full benefits of the Pax Romana was Jewish Palestine. There, after a short period of relative calm under the vassal Herod I (37–4 B.C.E.), the peace was interrupted incessantly by opposition to imperial rule, culminating in a wave of revolt and brutal suppression. Yet the catastrophic nature of these disturbances should not be unduly stressed, since even after the great uprising of 67–70, which ended in Titus's destruction of the Temple, the populations of Judea and Galilee remained predominantly Hebraic and economic conditions were basically unaltered.

It was not until almost a century later, following the Bar Kochba revolt, that the foundations of Jewish material civilization in Palestine lay shattered—but by that time the Imperial Peace itself was showing signs of breaking down.

Though Palestine continued as the core of the Jewish world for most of this period, some of the Diaspora communities were beginning to overshadow the motherland in economic importance, and Jewish adventurers were active far beyond the Roman Empire's frontiers.

In his celebrated tract *Of the Populousness of Ancient Nations* David Hume was one of the first modern writers to examine the tremendous difficulties in making reasonable estimates of population figures and trends in antiquity; as he pointed out, "the facts, delivered by ancient authors, are either so uncertain or so imperfect as to afford us nothing positive in this matter" (E. Rotwein, ed., *David Hume: Writings on Economics* [Edinburgh, 1955], p. 147). Although much fresh demographic evidence has come to light since Hume's day, the data remain highly empirical and the inferences drawn by leading authorities continue to display wide variations.

One such difference of opinion concerns the size of the Jewish people in the early Roman Empire, with J. Beloch estimating it at more than 6 million (out of a total population of about 60 million), while A. Harnack's computation is only 4.5 million. Even on the basis of the most conservative assessments, Israel, numerically at any rate, had become a far more important factor in the world than in biblical times. At the zenith of Roman prosperity, out of every thousand persons in the principate at least seventy were Jews—the proportion may have been as high as a hundred in every thousand; certainly, the percentage was considerably greater than in the present-day United States.

Early Jewish coins

The assessments for Palestine itself vary even more, with a figure of between 1.5 and 2 million at the time of Herod seeming to be reasonably near the mark, followed by fairly rapid depopulation during and after the insurrections. It is virtually certain that by the beginning of the second century more than twice as many Jews lived in other Roman provinces than in the mother country itself.

For the communities residing outside the Roman Empire, the sources are even less numerous and more dubious. Although the Greek geographer Strabo believed that "it is hard to find a place in the habitable earth that hath not admitted this tribe of men" (quoted in Josephus, *Antiquities*, 14.7.2 [in Whiston's translation, Boston, 1811]), and the historian Philo (himself Jewish) described "the continents full of Jewish colonies" (Philo Judaeus, *The Embassy to Gaius*, 36. 281–82 [in Yonge's translation, London, 1855]), the total figure for Persia, Babylonia, and the territories farther afield was probably not more than 1 million.

A notable distinction between Palestinian Jewry and the Diaspora settlements at this time was that, while the former remained predominantly rural, the latter were concentrated in urban areas. Jerusalem, with a population around 100,000, was by far the largest homeland city, though it was considerably smaller than coastal centers like Gaza, which were inhabited mainly by Greek and other non-Hebraic elements.

On the other hand, considerable Jewish minorities were now to be found in the great commercial centers of Asia Minor and Syria (such as Miletus, Sardis, Antioch, and Damascus), in the Aegean (especially at Delos), on the Greek mainland (Athens and Corinth), at Cyrene on the North African coast, in Sicily at Syracuse, and in Italy itself (at Rome and the port of Puteoli). In the new city of Seleucia (on the Euphrates north of Babylon) there were 50,000 Jews by the middle of the first century of the Christian Era; Alexandria, with its

200,000 Jewish citizens out of a total of about 500,000 inhabitants, had become, according to Mommsen, "almost as much a city of the Jews as of the Greeks" (Theodor Mommsen, *The Provinces of the Roman Empire* [London, 1909], 2:163).

Nevertheless, the Jews of Palestine remained essentially an agricultural people, and farming itself showed some marked advances over the situation prevailing in biblical times. Although the soil compared unfavorably with many of the more fertile regions of the empire, the increasing pressure of population (until the trend was reversed by the Judeo-Roman War) had promoted intensive, capitalistic methods of cultivation and costly artificial irrigation projects. This had resulted in improved yields of the staple grain products, wheat and barley, so that in good years there was sufficient to support the local population, meet demands for tributes from Rome, and provide small surpluses for commercial export. The best wheat grew near Mikmash in Judea, while the barley of Bethmakleh in the Kidron Valley was well known in overseas markets.

Orchard products, however, were very much more important as export items, and the wealthier citizens of the far-flung Roman domains were eager customers for Palestinian dates and figs, oil from the prolific olives of Gischala, and high-quality wines from the vineyards of Galilee. Balsam, with its medicinal qualities, was found only in the district around Jericho and was so highly prized that the destruction of the balsam plantations became a powerful economic weapon during the war against the Romans.

The Sea of Galilee supported a major fishing industry, with its salted and dried fish products being sold not only throughout Palestine but in markets abroad. In the drier eastern districts pastoral farming prevailed, as in former times, but many of the shepherds and cowherds had now become commercial cattlemen, making regular visits to the large meat and wool markets of Jerusalem.

Although a class of wealthy landed proprietors had come into being in Herodian times (many members of whom enjoyed connections with the ruling house or belonged to influential priestly families), independent peasant yeomen prevailed over most of the country, and the large estate (or latifundium) that had become so characteristic of rural organization in most parts of the Roman Empire was a comparatively rare phenomenon in Palestine. This stemmed partly from the fact that since Maccabean times the rabbinical enactments against debt bondage and the protection of gentile slaves (which surpassed even biblical legislation) had been rigidly enforced; and without a considerable supply of unfree labor the latifundia were not economically feasible.

In part, too, the absence of large estates flowed from the continued observance of scriptural laws, such as those concerning land redistributions in jubilee years. Yet the strict adherence to such moral injunctions became progressively more difficult for a farming community that had also to comply with Roman civic duties. As the ravages of revolt were superimposed on these burdens, rural prosperity tended to coexist with and then was replaced by extreme agrarian poverty.

Handicraft industry probably occupied a more important place in the Palestinian economy during the Imperial Peace than it had done in former times, in spite of the fact that the products of Jewish artisans were not able to compete with many imported wares, even when these were common items of everyday use, such as sandals, felt hats, and handkerchiefs. Nonetheless, the literature of the period mentions at least forty different types of native craftsmen, and there were many villages that had come to be associated with particular occupations. Textiles offered the most scope for industrial employment, with linen manufacturing being carried on chiefly in Galilee because of local flax supplies and woolen goods being produced mainly in Judea.

The dignity and blessing of manual labor was continually stressed in the scriptural commentaries, so there was little idleness, and many members of the priestly class as well as eminent scholars supported themselves and their families by manual toil: Hillel the Elder was employed as a woodcutter, Rabbi Nehunya was a well-digger, Rabbi Yehudah a baker, Jesus of Nazareth earned his living as a carpenter, and his disciple Paul was a tent-cloth weaver. Most crafts were passed on from father to son and were organized by guilds. Moreover, the rigid prohibitions against admitting gentiles into holy places fostered certain branches of industry, particularly construction work, and even the irreligious Herod was compelled to use only Jewish masons—some ten thousand of them—during his additions to the Temple.

The position of Palestine in the Roman world meant that many of the great international trade routes linking the east with Rome and the provinces of the far west traversed the country. This traffic was of sufficient volume to induce the Roman authorities to establish customhouses at Jericho, Caesarea, Jaffa, and Gaza, although much of this transit business, like the port cities themselves, was in non-Jewish hands. On the other hand, in return for the many natural products that the country itself exported, Palestine received foreign goods of wide variety and origins, ranging from Median beer and Edomite vinegar to Italian furniture and Corinthian candlesticks. These imports for the most part were handled by Jewish-owned caravans made up of Jewish donkey- and camel-drivers and seagoing ships manned by Jewish sailors.

Even merchants who had no contacts with the outside world frequently established commercial relations with the

Diaspora through the pilgrim trade that annually attracted many thousands of Jewish visitors to Jerusalem. In this way the capital became the center of a flourishing tourist industry, while the financial needs of the travelers brought into being a new class of specialist money changers and bankers, who set up their booths on the outskirts of the Temple. (Thus when Jesus "overthrew" their tables, Matt. 21:12, he was interfering with certain amenities that for the sake of convenience had become attached to the holy shrine.)

The Temple authorities themselves had come to depend on such banking services, since agents were needed to transfer the numerous endowments bequested by wealthy coreligionists throughout the empire and in Babylonia. Within the country full-time bankers collected the half-shekel that every adult contributed annually for the shrine's upkeep, transmitting the proceeds to Jerusalem for a small commission.

This was a comparatively mild tax compared to the exactions of the lay authorities. Herod himself, widely recognized as one of Rome's richest vassals, had built palaces and sanctuaries not only in Palestine but all over the eastern Mediterranean, and such splendor was achieved through a fiscal reign of terror. Yet the notoriety of the king's tax farmers was eclipsed by that of the Roman procurators who followed, although their levies on the users of roads, water, houses, and salt were probably no greater than those extracted from the natives of other countries subject to Rome.

Even Vespasian's *fiscus Judaicus* was not an additional burden but merely the transfer of the Temple tax to finance the erection of a pagan shrine in Rome. However, it was a grave religious affront, and insofar as political stability under foreign rule depended on the close coordination of priestly authority with local government, such Roman actions served to impair the country's economic well-being.

*   *   *

Although imperial rule in Palestine itself became increasingly oppressive, there remained many opportunities for personal advancement in the numerous Diaspora settlements. During the Pax Romana there was nothing to prevent an energetic Jewish citizen from rising in the armed services from the rank of common soldier to commander, or in administrative employment from petty official to a procuratorial post, even ending as a prefect. We know of at least one such case: Tiberius Julius, the historian Philo's nephew, became prefect of Egypt in the year 69 and played a prominent part in the behind-the-scenes activities that led to the appointment of Vespasian as emperor.

Others with the necessary drive and initiative gained a footing at the top of private enterprise, particularly in Alexandria, becoming "the most active traders of that great commercial metropolis" (H. H. Milman, *The History of the Jews* [Everyman's Library edition], 1:460), controlling the export trades in papyrus, wheat, and dates, and farming the public revenues for a contractual lump sum. Still others became important as craftsmen in the linen, silk, and metal industries, while the more recent arrivals in Egypt and the Asiatic provinces brought with them a detailed knowledge of the art of glassmaking. And in the Nile Delta, along the coast of Spain, and in other parts of the empire as well there were prosperous communities of Jewish commercial farmers.

Yet the few instances of opulence and great Jewish fortunes that are known of should not obscure the fact that the masses of the Diaspora often lived in dismal poverty. Even in wealthy Alexandria, Philo records the existence of dark, congested, unhealthy ghettolike quarters and a life pervaded by economic uncertainty. The colony in Delos mainly comprised petty tradesmen eking out a marginal subsistence. In Rome itself Juvenal made fun of the Jewish beggars whom he found swarming in the neighborhood of the sacred grove of Egeria. Indeed, all over the empire Jews were prominent among the flotsam of the large cities, earning meager livelihoods from manual labor and peddling, or resorting to such bizarre occupations as interpreting dreams and telling fortunes.

Of course, such economic rootlessness and poverty were by no means confined to Jews; they had become a common feature of urban life throughout an empire in which almost all jobs were monopolized by slave labor. But while the attention of the shiftless, unemployed mobs of Rome was occupied by costly bread-and-circus entertainments, for destitute Jews in Alexandria, Cyrene, and other east Mediterranean metropolitan centers the only diversion was the fostering of a bond of solidarity with their downtrodden coreligionists in the motherland. It was a situation that inevitably led to the widespread Diaspora uprisings of the years 115–17.

These unsettling events in the provinces, together with the increasing oppression of imperial rule in Palestine itself, induced some Jews to hazard their fortunes beyond the empire's boundaries. Following on the abortive revolt in Cyrene, for example, an important southward migration took place toward Senegal and the middle Niger, as a consequence of which Jews became widely scattered throughout the whole interior of North Africa and began to participate in the trans-Saharan caravan traffic. Meanwhile, the disturbances occasioned by the Jewish revolt in Alexandria not only greatly impaired the prosperity of that city, but also induced the emperor Trajan to bypass the port by building a canal from the Nile to Clysma on the Gulf of Suez.

This link between the Mediterranean and the Red Sea was now needed to facilitate a growing volume of maritime traffic with the Far East after the discovery of the monsoon's seasonal movements, which enabled shipping to make direct for

India instead of hugging the coastline. Jewish traders had been familiar with the products of oriental commerce ever since the Asiatic conquests of Alexander; linen and muslin fabrics of Indian origin had been imported regularly into Judea, while aromatic woods from Assam and China had reached the Hebrews via the Persian Gulf and Arabia. Accordingly, Jewish merchants were among the first to take part in the growing seaborne trade with the East, and by the close of the second century they were well established in Cochin on the Malabar coast, from which they probably built up commercial ties with the districts of Lu Shan and Tcheng-tu in China. Others traded at the mouth of the Indus, eventually penetrating into Afghanistan and founding a colony near Kabul.

However, the overland routes were not altogether neglected, and by the second century Jewish middlemen were sharing in the caravan silk traffic from China to Europe. Most of these merchants belonged to the Babylonian communities, which then formed part of the sprawling Parthian Empire. In addition to such participation in long-distance commerce, these Jews of the Euphrates Valley were commercial cattle breeders and, according to Graetz, carried on "trades of all descriptions" (Heinrich Graetz, *History of the Jews* [Philadelphia, 1893], 2:508). But few specific details of their economic activities have survived, although it would seem that they enjoyed a considerable degree of local autonomy and paid reasonable taxes.

Jewish economic life during the Imperial Peace, therefore, presents a checkered pattern: in the ancestral homeland it was a time of mounting anarchy accompanied by economic retrogression and emigration; beyond Palestine, while there were opportunities for material advancement for the enterprising or lucky few, the majority appear to have been unsettled and unprosperous. Yet in many respects Jewish experience in this era was a prelude in miniature for what was to overtake all the empire's peoples once the Pax Romana itself had collapsed.

II

THE
MEDIEVAL
PERIOD

4

BYZANTINE JEWRY AND
THE MEDIEVAL ECONOMY

Four centuries after the destruction of Jerusalem by Roman
legions under Titus, the city of Rome itself was destroyed by
Genseric the Vandal. Thereafter the focal point of both trade
and industry tended to shift to Constantinople, which had
become the capital of the East Roman or Byzantine Empire.
It was in this city of Constantine's, in the heart of the largest
Christian state of early medieval times, that Jewish merchants and manufacturers were to play roles of some historical significance.

Centuries before the Pax Romana a considerable Jewish
population had existed within the territory of what was to
become the Eastern Empire. Even after the rapid expansion
of Islam had detached the sizable communities in Egypt and
the Levant from Byzantine rule, by the ninth century there
remained something like a thousand Jewish settlements governed from Constantinople, notably in Macedonia, Thrace,
and Thessaly—though probably the ones in the capital itself
and in the industrial center of Thebes were the largest by far.

Because of the meagerness of surviving population statistics it is impossible to estimate even approximately the total
number of Jewish inhabitants of Byzantium during the early

Middle Ages, and one suggestion (it can be no more than an intelligent guess) that at the period of their greatest prosperity they numbered perhaps 150,000 in an empire of 15 million is misleading; the great majority of those 15 millions were self-sufficing peasants in various stages of serfdom whose economic activities had no importance beyond the boundaries of the farms on which they lived and worked. Hence even a small proportion of such a population—as few as 1 percent—could exert great influence if its energies were appropriately exercised.

In Constantinople itself, as early as the time of Justinian (mid-sixth century) the Jews were sufficiently numerous to have occupied a separate quarter called *Halkoprateia* ("the Brass Market"), which suggests that their segregation was based on occupational rather than religious grounds and that they at first specialized in the city's copper and brass industries. Later the majority seem to have lived in a suburb north of Galata, the principal business district.

While it would be idle to pretend that Byzantine Jewry was not subject to periodic bouts of persecution, during the greater part of medieval times most imperial edicts were more often concerned with protecting the Jews than impinging upon their freedom. Moreover, in strong contrast to the lands of the Christian West and the Muslim southeast, special taxes were rarely imposed on the Jewish communities of the Eastern Empire, and where discriminatory legislation did apply (such as the exclusion of Jews from the public service and the army) it operated against *all* persons not of the Greek Orthodox faith.

Even in early medieval times a document closely resembling the modern passport was required to cross frontiers and to be admitted to the main markets of the Muslim states, the Byzantine Empire, Lombard Italy, and the Carolingian domains. And as a rule only Jews could freely go back and forth between Europe and non-Christian lands without arousing suspicion, because they were strategically and politically harmless. (In fact, in Carolingian France they had become so predominant in trade by the ninth century that the surviving texts often divide traders into two classes, "the Jews and the other merchants.")

The advantages of this almost extraterritorial position were most pronounced in Constantinople itself. There the activities of foreign traders were carefully supervised by the city prefect: on arrival they had to report to his bureau, their purchases were carefully scrutinized to insure that customs regulations were not contravened, special lodgings were prescribed, and their stay was limited to a maximum of three months. Such limitations were imposed mainly for security reasons. However, since this security problem did not arise in the case of Jewish traders, it meant that even those who were not normally residents of the empire did not have their movements circumscribed in these ways and that no time limit was imposed on the length of their stay.

The Jewish merchants of Byzantium participated in three principal areas of far-flung commerce. First, there was the Far Eastern trade, in which Jewish adventurers carrying bullion traveled to Damascus, Baghdad, and Basra to procure spices, raw silk, and other oriental luxuries for disposal on the entrepôt market of Constantinople. Some went farther afield in their search for Eastern wares, going to India and China both overland and by sea, thereby maintaining a Jewish commercial tradition that dated back to the centuries of the Imperial Peace and preceded the travels of Marco Polo the Venetian by more than four centuries.

Their second sphere of operations lay north of Byzantium, through the lands of the Magyars, Bulgars, and Khazars, in the direction of Kiev; there they made contact with the

Swedish Varangians then active along the Volga and Dnieper, from whom they purchased honey, wax, furs, and amber, giving spices and articles of Byzantine manufacture in exchange. Extreme climatic conditions—especially the winter freeze-ups of the Russian rivers—made trading in this area difficult and hazardous.

Third, there were the markets of the West. The Byzantine emperors still exercised nominal control over several cities in Italy, of which Amalfi and Venice were the most important, and certainly until the tenth century much of the commerce passing through these outposts of the industrial East were handled by Jewish businessmen who maintained close ties with Constantinople. During the Carolingian era Marseilles regained some of its former importance through a lively seaborne traffic with Byzantium in papyrus, textiles, and wine, in which Jewish entrepreneurs again played a leading part. In Spain, too, Jewish traders were regular importers of Byzantine cloths into the kingdom of León.

Thus in spite of the difficulties entailed in trade with distant places in early medieval times, Jewish merchants were often instrumental in enabling the Constantinople entrepôt to keep the Occident in economic touch with the Orient.

While much of the Byzantine traffic that these traders handled comprised reexports of foreign origin, some local industries also served an international market, and of these the most important was the manufacture of silken textiles.

Each guild in this industry enjoyed a monopoly over a particular branch or grade of silk production, but all were subject to rigorous supervision by the state authorities, who fixed the level of profits, laid down conditions for the admission of new members, placed restrictions on the exportation of certain types of cloth (to keep up prices), and even specified the localities where workshops could be established.

Although we lack any detailed information, it seems that

the majority of those Jews who were not engaged in some aspect of foreign commerce worked in the silk industry or the closely associated dyeing trade. In view of their pronounced religious character, it is unlikely that the silk guilds of Constantinople and Thebes would readily have admitted Jewish members. How, then, did these Jewish craftsmen fit into the system of guild monopoly and state control? It is well known that from the late tenth century on, in many towns of Western Europe where guilds were formed Jewish craftsmen, being unable to gain admission, set up a kind of guild of their own. The same sort of thing appears to have happened at a somewhat earlier date in Byzantium. Wherever the number of skilled Jewish artisans in a particular branch of the silk industry warranted it, a Jewish closed shop would evolve to provide them with an organizational framework, control competition among members, regulate the admission and number of journeymen and apprentices, supervise quality of output, negotiate with government officials, and make adjustments of policy in accordance with varying pressures from Christian rivals.

No doubt the Jews of Byzantium also followed a variety of other industrial occupations, and they almost certainly figured prominently among the ranks of the goldsmiths and jewelers in Constantinople. But the absence of data about such pursuits reinforces the impression that, besides foreign trade, their main employment was in the silk industry.

The advent of the Crusades put an end to this socially tolerable and economically prosperous state of affairs. When the Fourth Crusade was diverted to Constantinople by the Venetians in 1204, it was the Jewish quarter that fell first, and a large part of its population was butchered. Thereafter the new crusader-dominated regime consistently followed a virulent anti-Jewish policy.

Constantinople itself, after sack and pillage by the crusaders, was a ruin of the city it had once been. The restoration of the Byzantine Empire in 1261 did not mean a return to prosperity for those Jews who had survived the crusader persecutions; the state itself, weakened by loss of territory, financial instability, and the further spread of serfdom, was now racked by an economic palsy from which it never recovered.

It was only much later, after the complete disappearance of Byzantium when southeastern Europe was overrun by the Ottoman Turks, that the Jewish community of Constantinople regained its economic importance.

Moreover, it is one of the ironies of history that eventually the city's Jews outnumbered its Christian inhabitants (the community's ranks having been reinforced by refugees from the Iberian persecutions). In 1554, when Hans Dernschwam, a trusted employee of the leading south German business house of the Fuggers, visited the Bosphorus, he noted that the current tax list contained the names of fifteen thousand adult male Jews but less than seven thousand Christians, although all non-Muslim groups were obliged to pay tribute to the sultan. This observant German traveler wrote in his diary: "In Constantinople, the Jews are as thick as ants, and there are no wares which they do not carry about and trade in. . . . There are also all sorts of artisans among their ranks," and Dernschwam's list included printers, goldsmiths, engravers, mirror-makers, as well as the traditional silk-workers and dyers.

So the Byzantine Empire had managed to outlive its Western (Roman) counterpart by a thousand years, but the Jews of Constantinople had displayed even more resilient qualities of survival.

5

JEWISH TRADERS
IN THE MEDIEVAL
MEDITERRANEAN WORLD

Until the present century there was something of a missing link in the story of widespread trade relations between the western and eastern halves of Europe during the early Middle Ages—that is, roughly, from the time of the Muslim inroads to the beginning of the Crusades (c. 700–1100). For instance, the historian Heyd asks: "By what means did the peoples of the northwest procure eastern products before and during the Crusades? Here is a problem which demands solution and which is more difficult than is at first apparent" (W. Heyd, *Histoire du commerce du Levant au moyen-âge*, ed. F. Raynaud, 2 vols. [Leipzig, 1886], 2:727).

The main problem was that the sources of information are extremely scanty. Practically no commercial documents of the eighth and ninth centuries have survived, and contemporary chroniclers paid little attention to economic matters. In the absence of adequate data, widely different evaluations of the nature and volume of early medieval trade were formulated, ranging from the extreme optimism of Alfons Dopsch to the pessimistic writings of Henri Pirenne. Nonetheless, archeological delvings (such as the unearthing of hoards of coin), occasional remarks in agrarian and legal documents,

and incidental comments scattered about in the extant official and semiofficial compilations of the period gradually enabled scholars like J. Brutzkus and W. J. Fischel to fill in at
least a part of the gap. And their inquiries clearly suggest that
Jewish merchants handled a very considerable share of early
medieval commerce.

One of the earliest accounts of Jewish trade across the
Mediterranean to the Far East is to be found in *The Book of
Roads and Governments* compiled in the mid-ninth century
by the Arab official responsible for postal arrangements in
the caliphate of Baghdad. He records how Jewish travelers,
embarking from the ports of southern France, would carry
cargoes of slaves, brocades, and furs to the marts of Constantinople, Alexandria, and Damascus. The more venturesome
would then proceed by caravan across the Fertile Crescent
and sail from the Persian Gulf for India and China, to return
with "musk, aloe, wood, camphor, cinnamon, and other products of the eastern countries" for distribution in the lands of
the West.

Another Arabic work, *The Wonders of India,* written
about 953, recounts the story of a Jewish merchant prince
who "left Oman without owning anything and came back on
his own ship laden with musk worth a million dinars, silken
stuffs, and porcelain of an equal value, jewels and precious
stones for at least as much, to say nothing of a heap of won-
derful things from China."

In the remoter hinterlands of the Mediterranean, such as
the interior provinces of France, these traders appear to
have held almost a monopoly of international commerce—so
much so that the words *"Judaeus"* and *"mercator"* appear as
synonyms in Carolingian documents. And it was only
through their efforts that the Christian church was able to
procure incense and the rich vestments that had become
essential for religious services and the upholding of ecclesias-

tical offices. Although these Jewish merchants had rivals in the more advanced Byzantine and Muslim lands, even in those territories they were second to none in the scope and importance of their travels in search of commercial profits.

The reasons for their preeminence are not difficult to discover: like all successful medieval traders they were good linguists ("These merchants speak Arabic, Persian, Roman, Frankish, Spanish, and Slavonic"); they displayed a business acumen far in advance of the times, making use of both credit instruments and partnership agreements, thereby spreading the heavy risks of loss while goods were in transit and hedging to some extent against price uncertainties in Western markets; equally important, their perpetual travels gave them an expert knowledge of the principal land and sea routes and of the many hazards to be encountered and overcome while spices and other precious luxury articles were laboriously transported from supply sources to consumption centers—not for nothing were they known as Radanites, from the Persian for "one who knows the way" *(rah dan)*.

Most significant of all, however, was the fact that the prevailing enmity between the Christian West and the Muslim East provided tremendous scope for the entrepreneurial energies of Jewish middlemen.

Such commercial leadership could last only as long as Islam remained a direct menace to southern Europe. But by the close of the tenth century Arab political unity had been shattered, and with this fragmentation of the caliphates the Muslim threat to the communities along the northern shores of the Mediterranean began to recede. Since the dwindling of armed tension usually promotes a desire for closer economic contacts, Christian merchants began to contemplate the establishment of direct trade relations with Tunis, Egypt, and the Levant; for their part, the businessmen of Alexandria and

Aleppo were discovering that legitimate commerce could be a better means of accumulating wealth than plunder and piracy.

In fact, as early as the ninth century Jewish seaborne traffic had started to feel the effects of competition from the more advanced Italian maritime cities, such as Amalfi and Venice, whose merchants now vied with the Radanites as intermediaries between the dynamic economies of Byzantium and Baghdad and the relatively self-sufficient feudal-manorial lands of Central and Western Europe. And, by the time of the early Crusades, the Italians were mercilessly and successfully destroying Jewish trade along the Mediterranean sea-lanes.

Forced to succumb to more powerful rivals, many Jewish merchants were thus unwillingly compelled to concentrate their activities along the transcontinental river routes to the east, a shift that eventually led to the rise of important Jewish entrepôts at Mainz, Regensburg, and Prague.

Meanwhile, those Radanites who did not transfer to German and Slav territories were gradually compelled to confine their business operations to petty retailing, peddling, and moneylending. With the onset of the Crusades, however, even in these spheres they began to experience increasing competition from Christian pawnbrokers and usurers, such as the so-called Lombards (who were mainly Piedmontese from the Chieri district).

In fact, the Jewish mercantile class of Mediterranean Europe was practically the only group whose material welfare became progressively worse during the era of the Crusades, its declining fortunes being very largely a consequence of the tightening up of discriminatory measures. Previously there had been little sustained discrimination, since the Radanites were performing an indispensable function at a time when there was no other middleman group. By the eleventh century, however, native traders had learned to dispense with such services and started seeking their rivals' exclusion. Henceforth, Jews engaged in Mediterranean commerce survived by exception and privilege rather than by natural right.

One notable result of the Crusades was the shift from the Near East to the Italian mainland as the economic focal point of the Mediterranean world. The religion of Venice was a religion of astute businessmen, and that city waxed prosperous and powerful by exploiting crusader expeditions to serve its own ends. The Genoese became pioneers of new trading contacts with the Orient after Marco Polo had related his experiences in the lands of the great khans. In Florence tremendous wealth was amassed by drapers, whose cloth industry came to serve the needs of all southern Europe—wealth that was to be used to finance the great artistic and literary Renaissance centered on that city in the later Middle Ages. In short, these great commercial and industrial centers of Italy firmly set the pace for economic expansion. What role did Jewish enterprise play in this process and what was the status of those Radanites who had not migrated?

Of all medieval Mediterranean cities, Venice, with its cosmopolitan atmosphere, should have continued to provide a relatively favorable milieu for Jewish trading ventures. Hazlitt, for instance, observes: "We cannot too warmly admire and commend the unique indulgence extended to members of all creeds, Jews inclusive, on this soil" (W. Carew Hazlitt, *The Venetian Republic,* 2 vols. [London, 1900], 2:397). In reality, the Jews of Venice were in a peculiar position: although Radanites had been active in these Adriatic lagoons from the earliest times (often as agents for Constantinople business houses), and although their ranks had swollen to several thousands by the mid-twelfth century, they were not classified as citizens—in spite of the fact that many were permanent residents. Nor were they regarded as foreign merchants, because they did not come from their own trading area and were thus not entitled to a *fondaco* (or caravansary built and maintained by the state), such as visiting German merchants of the Hanseatic League possessed.

Hence, the surviving records indicate that whenever a conflict of interests arose, the promulgation of more and more discriminatory injunctions was the inevitable consequence. A typical instance is the following report from the Venetian governor of the Retimo district, who had been receiving complaints from the local citizens: "They have explained that the Jews, not content with the interest and incalculable profit that they obtain from usuries, capture all proceeds that are obtained from the art and profession of commerce, so much so that one could say that these very Jews are lords of the money and of the men of that locality; and further, that these very Jews occupy nearly all the stalls, shops, and stores, both those located on the square of Retimo and those around and near the square; and this brings very great harm upon our faithful and their utter destitution, because only these very Jews sell and dispose of their merchandise, and our citizens, being unable to have the said shops, are not able to sell anything or have any proceeds." The upshot of such agitation was that Jewish merchants were progressively confined to restricted areas of trade, forced to subscribe to compulsory loans, and subjected to periodic expulsions.

Their status was probably even more precarious in the great rival city of Genoa, whose modern beginnings were deeply rooted in campaigns against the Muslims in home waters; much of the religious intolerance generated during those formative decades was subsequently transferred to the Jews. Thus, as Theodore Bent has pointed out in his history of the Genoese republic, "they were liable at any moment to be hunted out of house and home, and sent forth into the world as beggars" (J. Theodore Bent, *Genoa: How the Republic Rose and Fell* [London, 1881], p. 19). Consequently, although there were prosperous individual Jewish businessmen to be found in medieval Genoa, the community as a whole existed on the margin of popular forbearance.

And in the industrial metropolis of Florence, where all social and political life was dominated by a few families of powerful merchant-drapers who controlled the city's intricate guild structure—there, too, Jewish merchants were never an integral part of economic development. They were subject to very strict limits on the interest they charged for loans (regardless of the risks involved); they were restricted residentially, denied citizenship rights, forbidden to carry arms, and excluded entirely from participating in the city's enormous foreign wholesale trade. The very fact that they could be segregated without causing any serious dislocation of Florentine economic life suggests that the presence of Jewish traders was of relatively little consequence.

The available evidence indicates, therefore, that Jewish enterprise in medieval Italy was never vital or even moderately important to the continuity and further expansion of commercial activities. Having helped very materially to initiate the reawakening of trade across the Mediterranean world, the Jews now found themselves ousted by those native rivals who were in a position to direct political and religious pressure against them—a phenomenon that was to be repeated in the lands of Western Europe during the later Middle Ages.

6

JEWISH ECONOMIC ACTIVITIES
IN MEDIEVAL ISLAM

Although the differences between the Roman Empire and medieval Islam may have been very great, the parallels and similarities are even more striking. Both endured lacerating civil wars followed by golden ages; both were sustained by a constant infusion of new blood; and both succumbed to blows from well-intentioned saviors which were meant to cure. But above all both empires enriched themselves at the expense of dependent peoples. Commodities that had once flowed to Rome and other centers of extravagant consumption in the West subsequently flowed to comparable centers, such as Cairo and Damascus, in the East.

Just as the Jews had played a significant role in the economic life of the Roman world during the Imperial Peace, so also were they to play their part in the evolving material civilization of the Arab communities in the Middle Ages. The appearance of the first volume of Prof. S. D. Goitein's trilogy, *A Mediterranean Society*, an event of momentous importance, focuses a powerful light on some aspects of Jewish business life in medieval Islam.

The work is based on a careful scrutiny and analysis of the rich hoard of Jewish documents found in the Cairo geniza.

Such places were once very numerous. In effect, they were gigantic repositories where papers of every kind ended up after they had ceased to be of any value to their owners, although they were still regarded as sacred because they were written in Hebrew and bore the name of God. Their contents, accordingly, were enormously diversified and thus of tremendous value to the economic historian.

The Cairo geniza, originally an annex of the Old Cairo synagogue, became a priceless archive after its rediscovery during renovations in 1890, and the bulk of its contents have now been acquired by libraries in Israel, Europe, and the United States. Its earliest manuscripts are ninth- and tenth-century ones, but the bulk concern the period from the beginning of the eleventh to the middle of the thirteenth centuries.

It was during the era of the Fatimid caliphate—centered on Egypt but maintaining close ties with Baghdad and Cordova—that the authorities made copious use of Jewish organizational abilities, and professing Jews were to be found in the highest positions in the Fatimid administration.

Factories, in the modern sense of large workshops employing many workers to turn out mass-produced goods, rarely appear in the geniza records, just as big industry was unknown in ancient Rome. Only two occupations seem to have been carried on, at least in part, on a large scale: sugar refining and the manufacture of paper. For the rest, the usual form of production was the small workshop, run by a single Jewish craftsman (sometimes he had a partner), with the assistance of his family.

Scanning these records the modern reader is impressed by the great number of separate occupations they reveal (no fewer than 265), indicating a high degree of specialization. As in Byzantium, Jews in medieval Islam were preeminent in the silk industry—by far the most valuable branch of textile production—though they by no means held a monopoly on the trade. The preparation of flax and the weaving of linen were also highly significant.

Jewish goldsmiths and silversmiths were very active; another branch of this craft was that of the "maker of ornaments," including all kinds of jewelry. In everyday life the products of these craftsmen occupied a position quite different from the one they have nowadays: besides their function as ornaments, they served largely as a means of investment and savings.

The testimony of the geniza records also point to glass manufacturing as a favorite Jewish occupation, possibly because the elaborate dietary and purity laws could be more easily observed with the use of glass vessels. The tanning of leather, bookbinding, and the preparation of foodstuffs (especially bread and pastries) appear to have been other major sources of Jewish industrial employment.

Regularity of work seems to have been a feature of Jewry in Islam, for none of the geniza records refer to an artisan's being without work; on the contrary, they suggest that it was not always easy to hire the services of a craftsman. Perhaps one reason for this absence of unemployment in the modern sense is that even a craftsman with small means or none at all would not, as a rule, become a wage earner; instead, he would enter into partnership with one or more fellow craftsmen or with an outsider who would provide him with capital.

In spite of the maritime growth of the Italian cities, Mediterranean commerce remained predominantly in Islamic hands during the eleventh century, and it was natural that Arabic-speaking Jews should have held a fair share of such trading activities. In the following century, when European naval supremacy became paramount, the geniza documents indicate that the Jewish merchants of Islam sought an alternative outlet for their enterprise by trafficking with the countries of the Indian Ocean.

About two hundred items of the far-flung oceanic trade recur in geniza records, around forty of which must be regarded as being of major importance, including dyestuffs, textile piece goods, herbs, and wine. But to all intents and purposes the Arabic-speaking Jewish merchants of the Mediterranean area (with the possible exception of those in Sicily and Spain) confined their activities to the realms of Islam. Although there are scattered references to business trips to Constantinople, Amalfi, Genoa, Marseilles, and other Christian ports, it is clear that such voyages were not regular and were not undertaken by a great number of merchants.

The reason for this was that, as a rule, Europeans made their way to the markets of Tunisia, Egypt, and the Levant, and Arabic-speaking merchants seldom transported goods to Europe. Thus although Islamic Jewry was connected with its coreligionists in Europe by bonds of general culture, religion, and philanthropy, there were few business relations of any significance.

Even then only the bigger merchants would engage in long-distance trade (such as between Tunis and Alexandria) with all the hazards it involved. The rank and file, which form the bulk of the people represented in the geniza documents, voyaged from one market to its nearest neighbor, moving on only when they were not able to sell any more of their stock or buy what they were after. Moreover, the geniza papers tend to confirm what many modern economic historians now believe—that medieval commerce at its peak was great only in comparison with that of earlier periods; when compared with commerce in the modern world it shrinks to a trickle. On the other hand, it has to be remembered that these merchants usually concluded a series of short-term partnerships with a number of correspondents, so that an account or a letter, with its details about the quantity and value of goods, generally reflects only a portion of the transactions entered into during a given period.

In an age of erratic marketing contacts, the pull of monopoly profits was always a strong one (as it was among the merchant guildsmen of Christian Europe), and when a convoy of foreign vessels reached harbor it was inevitable that some of the local Jewish traders would try to buy all the imports and force up prices. A letter from Alexandria contains the following report: "Six Venetian ships have arrived with a great mass of precious goods. However, our coreligionists monopolized everything that came in them, thus providing exorbitant profits for the Venetians and doing pernicious things never experienced before in the customhouse."

There is no specific word for "Mediterranean" in these geniza records—it is simply referred to as "The Sea"; as long as one traveled on it one was, so to speak, within one's own precincts and never beyond reach. A merchant from Bône (in Algeria) who wanted to collect an outstanding debt in Cairo a few days prior to the due date pretended that he was traveling to Yemen; as soon as it became obvious that he had departed for Algeria instead, the debtor was furious: "Had I known that he was going only to the West, I would not have paid him a thing."

On the other hand, a debtor in Cairo who was unable to meet his commitments fled to a port on the Red Sea coast, since the Mediterranean was much too frequented to provide a safe refuge. Commuting regularly between the western and eastern halves of the Mediterranean basin was a humdrum experience: "I am astonished that he has not come around Passover, as he is accustomed to do," says a letter from Alexandria with regard to a Tunisian merchant.

The geniza records reveal, too, that not only merchants but also craftsmen traveled extensively: many Jewish artisans in Tunisia, for instance, bore Persian names. Egypt during the eleventh and twelfth centuries attracted large numbers of glassmakers and dyers from Palestine, while the records indicate that silversmiths from Ceuta, Morocco, emigrated via Aden as far as Ceylon.

This constant movement of craftsmen from one part of the Islamic world to another was a major factor in the diffusion of industrial arts. Mobility of persons, products, and ideas became the hallmark of Islamic economic life in the High Middle Ages, and references to limitations and obstacles to such movements are conspicuously absent in the geniza papers.

Not only was there much geographical movement but also many occupational shifts, as individual Jews improved their social status or became proficient specialists. Thus we read about a physician whose father was a fishmonger, while the proprietor of a seagoing vessel carrying large cargoes started off his business career as a vendor of bananas. And in many cases the records list persons bearing names associated with manual occupations (like potters, saddlers) in the capacity of traders of high-priced goods, such as spices. In contrast to the rigid, static nature of European society at that time, such opportunities for individual economic advancement are noteworthy. In medieval Islam, natural gifts and aptitudes rather than status at birth determined one's place in society.

The geniza documents, then, illustrate a society in which men, goods, money, and books traveled almost without restriction throughout the Islamic Mediterranean world. In fact, the area was close to being a free-trade community, with remarkably liberal treatment of foreigners. They certainly show, too, that the taste for expensive luxury and novelty articles did not vanish from the Mediterranean with the fall of Rome and the disintegration of the Western empire.

These documents also indicate that the close connections among all parts of the Jewish Diaspora—expressed in contributions to, and spiritual and organizational dependence upon, ecumenical religious authorities in distant countries—were not regarded by the Arab governments of the various states concerned as being in any way an infringement on their sovereignty.

In contrast to medieval Christian Europe of the crusader era, where discriminatory restrictions were confining Jews to a few unproductive occupations, the world reflected in these geniza records was one offering much scope to Jewish professional specialists, craftsmen, and merchants.

7

THE JEWISH MONEYLENDERS
OF ROUSSILLON

During the twelfth and thirteenth centuries the Jews of southern France and the Spanish borderlands played a significant role in the economic life of that area—the community of Montpellier being especially prominent. But the classic surveys of this field (such as those by Jean Regné and Gustave Saige), though helpful, were defective and misleading in that they made little or no use of notarial registers, thereby leaving the impression that the Jews of Languedoc and adjacent territories differed little from their Christian neighbors in economic activities and interests.

Of course very few of these medieval registers have survived, but a recent study of seventeen volumes of notarial records of the town of Perpignan for the years 1261–87 provides a body of evidence substantial enough to throw much-needed light on a number of hitherto obscure problems.

Perpignan, the county seat of Roussillon (then part of the kingdom of Aragon), was a typical product of the mid-thirteenth-century commercial and urban revival: not only had it become a center of woolen cloth production and a junction for the overland trade routes from Barcelona to Marseilles and the Champagne fairs, it had also benefited greatly from the decline of neighboring Narbonne, which no longer enjoyed easy access to the sea owing to the silting up of its harbor.

Like all towns with a mushrooming commerce and industry, at first Perpignan must have experienced a relative shortage of capital, and for a time there was a marked differential in interest rates prevailing there and in the older Languedocian centers. It seems likely, therefore, that the movement of Jews from Languedoc to Roussillon that got under way in the thirteenth century was very largely a movement of capital seeking a higher rate of return.

About 1280, Perpignan Jewry comprised approximately one hundred families and had become one of the largest and most influential communities north of the Pyrenees. (It should be remembered that few medieval towns housed more than ten thousand persons, so that with something like four hundred inhabitants, the Jewish community must have accounted for at least 5 percent of the total population.) It was intimately tied to the Jewries of southern France and northern Spain by personal, economic, and intellectual connections, and some of its members had accumulated very sizable fortunes.

How did these Jews support themselves? To what extent did they earn their living by trade, through the production of goods, and in the various professions? In spite of the thriving commerce centered on the town, the notarial registers suggest that, with one or two minor exceptions, the Jews of Perpignan were not concerned directly with foreign trade. Similarly, there is a notable absence of evidence in these records that they were at all active in selling goods on the local market. Although there was at least one Jewish commission agent who made a living by hawking goods for others, the records indicate that only a negligible fraction of the community was supported by craft activities. Nor is there any indication that Jews were to be found among the professional groups (such as medical doctors or scribes).

The evidence is overwhelming that this rather substantial group of Jews supported itself by moneylending, to the virtual exclusion of all other economic activities. Of the 228 adult male Jews mentioned in the registers, almost 80 percent appear as lenders to their Christian neighbors. Nor were loans by Jewish women (mostly widows) uncommon, and the capital of minors was often invested in a similar manner. Moreover, those Jews most active as moneylenders appear to have been the most respected members of the community; Menahem Meiri, a distinguished rabbi and scholar, appears in the documents as a moneylender in no fewer than thirty-one transactions, and the names of the local Jewish poets, Pinhas Hal-Levi and Abram Bedersi, appear in that capacity too. In short, Perpignan Jewry paid its royal taxes, bought its food, clothing, and other necessities from the Christian populace, and supported its own communal institutions very largely out of the profits of moneylending.

Who borrowed money from the Jews of Perpignan in the thirteenth century? The answer appears to be, almost everyone—all ranks of Christian society are represented in the records as borrowers, including courtiers of the royal household, feudal knights, and individual members of the clergy; even some of the surrounding monastic abbeys (forced into temporary indebtedness by royal and papal taxation) found short-term Jewish credit useful.

The local townsmen accounted for about one-third of the loans for which there are records. Some of these people were agricultural laborers who worked on the surrounding estates, but probably most of the credit extended to this group took the form of pawnbroking loans and thus escaped being recorded; similarly, the two largest groups of artisans, the fullers and weavers (who operated on a piecework basis for

merchant drapers), appear to have done most of their borrowing on pawn. The cloth dealers themselves were prominent among the moneylenders' customers; these people
were heavily involved in credit operations, and at any given
moment might have large debts with suppliers, be owed
considerable amounts by customers, and have very little cash
on hand. Under such circumstances, it was only natural for
them to depend on short-term Jewish loans.

Loans to surrounding villagers make up more than half the
moneylending transactions in the surviving registers. Most of
these peasants borrowed without security, indicating a relatively high level of prosperity in the rural areas around Perpignan, but suggesting, too, that such people were regarded
as good risks—presumably because they owned real estate.
Regular travel through the Roussillon countryside must have
been an integral part of the moneylending business, and this
is testified to by the pains taken by many Perpignan Jews to
obtain letters of royal protection and exemptions from local
customs and tolls.

Thus from the evidence the typical Jew of thirteenth-cen-
tury Perpignan was a specialist moneylender, financing urban businessmen, on occasion lending to nobles and clerics,
and following beaten paths to villages in which he had
worked up a clientele. When he died his capital went on
performing these useful functions in the Roussillon economy,
since any minor children would be supported by a continuation of loan activities on their behalf by their guardian, while
the wife's dowry would be restored to her in the form of loan
contracts.

One fact emerges clearly from the registers: Jewish lenders
operated their businesses as individual projects, and there
are no indications that they either combined their capital or
diversified their risks through formal partnerships to any sig-

nificant extent. When the sum desired by a borrower was too large (or perhaps too risky) for a single Jew, the borrower would commonly contract two or more loans with different lenders.

Another fact which emerges is that in the region of Perpignan during the second half of the thirteenth century very little land had passed into Jewish ownership: of the 1,643 debts owed by Christians to Jews that appear in these records, there are only 31 transactions in which Jews are concerned with landed property. It was not usual to take over a defaulting debtor's real estate, and in most instances it seems that the debtor himself sold the property and the purchaser paid off the debt. In other words, if Christian businessmen at that period were tempted to invest in landed wealth, their Jewish counterparts were not; the latter were subject to special royal taxes that forced them to seek higher rates of return than could be earned from such real estate investments.

And the return from their moneylending was high by modern standards. Although the crown prescribed a maximum rate of 20 percent interest per annum, this was usually exceeded, the real rate being disguised by a fictitiously high face value on each loan. The documents indicate that such moneylending activities involved considerable risks and that the proportion of bad debts even among the more select clientele was by no means negligible. In view of the expenses of the business, the relative shortage of liquid capital, and the high proportion of bad loans, a rate as low as the prescribed 20 percent would hardly have been economically feasible. Moreover, since the Perpignan registers demonstrate that Jews lent money to members of all classes, rural and urban, lay and clerical, rich and poor, the interest charged must have borne a very direct relationship to the prevailing market price of money.

There can be no doubt, however, that from the contemporary point of view the Jews of Perpignan were engaged in "usury." The word *usura* occurs frequently in many of these documents, but its meaning is *synonymous with interest* and indistinguishable in any way from it. As far as the theologians were concerned, usury exacted by a Jew was banned just as any other type of usury was, and under canon law Christians could bring suits before an eccleciastical court for the restitution of such usury. The church's difficulty lay in imposing this view upon the secular authorities. The rulers of Aragon, like many other medieval authorities, found it to be in their own interest to permit the Jews to engage in usury, and when Perpignan moneylenders were cited before ecclesiastical tribunals, their activities were usually defended by local government officials.

The prosperity of Perpignan Jewry did not continue into the fourteenth century. The moneylending business had been seriously disturbed by the Franco-Aragonese War of 1285, most of which was fought on the soil of Roussillon. Moreover, the community had been swollen by Jews expelled from southern France. Interest rates fell as Christian entrepreneurs, through expanding business operations, slowly corrected the relative shortage of capital. Now the business of moneylending was no longer sufficient to support the community, and an increasing proportion of the Perpignan Jews turned of necessity to other occupations; the moneylenders that were left were apparently well along the road to becoming pawnbrokers exclusively.

There is also ample evidence in the early fourteenth century of a less friendly attitude on the part of the crown, with their adoption of some French fiscal devices. The earlier pattern—royal favor combined with moderate exploitation —gave way to one of severe restrictions and very drastic exploitation. Greater attention to charges of illegal interest rates alleged by Christian debtors against Jewish creditors formed part of the new policy; conviction brought with it both restoration of monies to the debtor and fines to the king.

The Jewish community of Perpignan never recovered from these blows. Its economic decline continued unchecked; having been one of the wealthiest Jewish centers of Western Europe, it had become relatively poor by the beginning of the fifteenth century. Thereafter its difficulties were made worse by the swelling tide of religious persecution, and its existence came to an end with the expulsion of 1493.

8

WHEN THE JEWISH GOOSE STOPPED
LAYING GOLDEN EGGS

The roots of modern English Jewry do not penetrate very deeply into history. While several European nations were busy planting settlers in the New World, Cromwell's council of state was still considering a motion that "the Jews deservinge it may be admitted into this nation to trade and trafficke and dwel amongst us as providence shall give occasion." As Cecil Roth has pointed out, for nearly four centuries prior to the Cromwellian Commonwealth, England "disappears almost entirely from the horizon of the Jewish world" (*History of the Jews in England* [Oxford, 1941], p. 89), and there are no important links connecting the medieval and modern phases of Jewish settlement in that land. And just as Cromwell's advisers were not primarily moved by humanitarian leanings but were anxious to secure the services of financially skilled Dutch Jewish immigrants, so also the main cause of the enforced emigration during the Middle Ages was economic.

The second half of the thirteenth century witnessed a general deterioration in the status of many Jewish communities throughout Western Christendom—it was an era of ruthless exploitation and merciless expulsion. Yet on the Continent, where most central governments were still weak, the many attempted solutions to the "Jewish problem" had only limited results; the rulers of Europe as yet possessed neither the administrative machinery nor the necessary power to deal with their Jews on a national basis.

Across the Channel, however, the situation was somewhat different: the English monarchy had always held more than mere nominal powers, and the feudal barons had never enjoyed quite the same degree of local autonomy as their counterparts on the mainland. During the thirteenth century, especially, the trend toward royal absolutism made significant progress in England, which meant that the Jewish issue could be handled on a nationwide scale. Thus to Edward I (1272–1307) belongs the dubious distinction of being the first European ruler to lift the Jewish question out of the political melting pot by the simple device of wholesale (and virtually complete) expulsion—thereby creating a precedent that Ferdinand and Isabella of Spain were to follow on a much larger and more tragic scale two centuries later.

Yet the fifteen thousand Jews who were forced to leave their homeland for France and Flanders in 1290 were not banished because Edward's government had suddenly developed religious scruples and could no longer tolerate a non-Christian community numbering less than 1 percent of the total population. Although the promulgation of exile stated that "to the honour of the Crucified, we have caused the Jews to go forth from our realm," religion was only the excuse for measures to solve an intricate economic problem that could be disentangled in no other way.

In England, as elsewhere across Western Europe, the gradual emergence of an exchange economy during and after the eleventh century had created new problems of ethical behavior, paramount among them being moneylending for profit. As far as the ecclesiastical authorities were concerned, all self-respecting Christians should abide by the injunction found in the Book of Luke (6:35), "Lend, expecting nothing in return," and successive church councils had imposed stringent restrictions on "usury" (which in medieval times did not imply merely lending money at exorbitant rates of interest, but covered virtually every transaction in which more was received than had been paid out).

These measures against usury meant that the business of moneylending was legally confined to non-Christians, of whom the only representatives in medieval England were the Jews. This raises a question: From what source did these Jewish moneylenders originally acquire their loanable funds? The evidence in this connection is scanty, although Sir John Clapham has suggested that for a time the first settlers in England (who came in the wake of the Norman conquest) retained commercial connections with their coreligionists in France. Then as native merchants, who were organized into guilds that excluded aliens from membership, began to participate in overseas trade, these Jewish traders were forced to seek other channels for the investment of their accumulated funds.

Ousted from commerce, they also found it virtually impossible to join the ranks of the artisan class, since all manufacturing activities were in the exclusive hands of the craft guilds—bodies with close church ties and therefore not likely to allow "unbelievers" to gain technical proficiency by becoming apprentices or journeymen. Furthermore, the complex feudal-manorial landholding arrangements were an effective barrier to their becoming farmers. (In any event, it would have been extremely foolhardy for a Jew in the Middle Ages to desert the relative security of the city walls in favor of a rural existence where at any time he and his family could become the victims of village prejudice or the scapegoats for a local crop failure.) The moneylending business, therefore, was their obvious choice.

In this restricted economic field there was apparently no limit to the nature of the pledges that these Jewish financiers were prepared to accept—from the armor of impoverished knights to the books of university students. But most important of all, in return for immediate cash loans they secured rent charges on fixed property—that is, the right to receive for a limited period all or part of the revenues flowing from the building or farm in question. It was a type of investment not unlike today's mortgage arrangements on fixed security. Such transactions were recognized by the church and were not classified as usurious.

By the closing decades of the twelfth century the crown had come to realize that these energetic moneylenders represented a source of liquid wealth to which it could periodically have recourse through arbitrary taxes (tallages). It was an age of constant political and military crises: rebellious barons had to be suppressed, the royal domains in France called for costly policing, and the tribes across the Welsh border were always giving trouble. So the financial needs of the central treasury were invariably urgent, yet the Great Council (which came to be known as Parliament around 1240) was often slow and reluctant in sanctioning additional supplies, especially if these were not accompanied by constitutional concessions.

Under such circumstances it was only natural that a royal screw would start to turn on the Jewish moneylenders, who were, in any event, classified as serfs of the crown in the existing feudal hierarchy, so that the king held the right to tallage them at will. In the century preceding the expulsion such arbitrary taxes became a normal method of supplementing the royal treasury.

In order to maximize the Jews' financial usefulness to the crown, without at the same time killing the goose that made such tallages possible, Richard I systematized the collection of these golden eggs by establishing a special "chest" in each of the towns where Jewish moneylenders were active; duplicate contracts of all financial agreements entered into with Jews were to be deposited into these chests. In London itself a coordinating body, "the Exchequer of the Jews," was created to collate all this information and to give judgment in all cases in which Jewish transactions were somehow involved.

Not only did these arrangements provide royal officials with a comprehensively detailed picture of current Jewish business dealings so they could assess the tallages which the community could bear from time to time, they also yielded valuable data for the levying of inheritance taxes, since, because the Jew was a serf of the crown, the state was entitled to confiscate his entire estate at death. (In practice, death duties usually varied from one-half to one-third the value of an estate, since it was obviously in the royal interest to leave heirs with enough capital to continue business operations and thus not endanger future taxable profits.)

Until the middle of the thirteenth century this system seems to have been beneficial to both parties, though by no means equally so. About one-sixth of the total royal revenue was derived annually from Jewish tallages, in return for which communities of Jews were to be tolerated in some twenty-seven specified centers and placed under the direct protection of the crown.

Obviously, England's medieval Jewish community could continue serving as one of the pillars on which royal finance rested only if it was not overtaxed. But very heavy taxation was instituted when Henry III (1216–72), who came to the throne as a boy of nine, began to rule in his own capacity. During his minority the guardians of the realm had been content to levy annual tallages of four or five thousand marks, but these amounts were more than quadrupled during the middle decades of the century to help defray the cost of Henry's growing commitments.

As tallage followed tallage, the Jewish moneylenders were forced to start eating into their capital, and many were obliged to sell their bonds. For the most part, the third parties who now purchased these rent charges were the powerful earls, who were then in a position to force the petty barons (the Jews' former chief clients) to part with their lands.

In this way the hard-pressed Jewish financier appeared to have become the tool of feudal society's upper strata in its policy of expropriating the estates of the lesser nobility. It is not surprising, therefore, that during the civil disturbances of the early 1260s the special targets of the lesser baronial forces were the chests recording indebtedness to Jews or their creditors. As it became increasingly obvious that the royal milch cow was being sucked dry, the crown's interest in Jewish affairs took a new direction: if the great earls were to be allowed to secure more and more land through the purchase of bonds from impoverished Jewish moneylenders, the king's own position might ultimately be undermined. Once this fear was recognized in palace circles the reaction was swift: in the "Provisions of Jewry" it was laid down in 1269 that in the future no debts of any kind were to be contracted with Jews on the security of fixed property and all existing obligations of that nature were to be canceled immediately. It would seem, therefore, that Jewish loans to improvident property owners had become an issue of great national significance.

Since the lesser nobility and the urban burgesses had no security to offer except land or buildings, the Jewish community, traditionally barred from the normal fields of economic activity, was now deprived of its most important financial function through the rapacity of the crown itself. A tallage of less than a thousand marks was all that Edward I could raise when he succeeded his father to the throne in 1272, and it was apparent that Jewish funds were no longer of any major significance in royal financial affairs. But worse was to come: in 1274 Pope Gregory X had urged Christendom to eradicate usury of every kind, and the new king took immediate steps to execute such a policy; an edict of the following year laid down that Jews (like Christians) were absolutely forbidden to lend money at interest and that all outstanding pledges were to be settled within six months.

This measure was the final step in Jewish financial disablement. The shrewd Edward, realizing that the usury prohibition would leave the Jewish community without employment, had relaxed the discriminatory laws in other directions, and Jews were now legally entitled to become merchants and artisans. But these apparently well-meant efforts at economic emancipation proved to be a series of empty gestures—the guilds were still much too powerful to accept passively even negligible inroads into their monopolies over urban industries and markets by a distrusted alien minority.

With the complete failure of Edward's experiment, a few Jews who had somehow managed to preserve a little working capital from the grasping fingers of the royal tax collectors switched their activities to the wholesale trade in raw wool, serving as intermediaries between the great monastic sheep farms and the exporters. A larger number tried to eke out a livelihood by selling plate or bullion fashioned from illegal clippings from the coinage. But the majority, wholly inexperienced in any other branch of economic activity, resorted to their traditional occupation of making usurious loans, using the same subterfuges that Christian moneylenders had been employing for decades to evade canon law.

Since circumstances had prevented Jewish economic assimilation and they were no longer capable of fulfilling their economic function of supplying the crown with ready funds whenever these were urgently needed, and since at the same time they were still a source of popular social and religious irritation, Edward had no alternative but to sweep away this problem of his father's making, which he had been unable to solve.

There was perhaps a little comfort in the news which these uprooted people heard some four years later after their wholesale deportation: that Edward's new Italian money-lenders had been unable to avert a grave royal financial crisis, and that to remain solvent the king had been obliged to grant important concessions to Parliament.

9

THE ECONOMIC BACKGROUND
TO THE EXPULSION
OF SPANISH JEWRY

On March 30, 1492, Ferdinand and Isabella, joint monarchs
of the recently united Christian kingdom of Spain, appended
their signatures to an edict that was to result in the cruelest
mass expulsion of Jews from any European territory in the
later Middle Ages. In most historical accounts of the circumstances surrounding this proclamation, it is invariably the
religious aspect of the issue that is stressed. Undoubtedly, the
violent campaign against heresy conducted by the Holy
Office and the fanaticism of the inquisitor-general, Tomás de
Torquemada (himself believed to have been of Marrano extraction) were the immediate influences on the crown's decision; but the situation was considerably more complex and its
roots were more deeply embedded in the soil of Spanish
history than is usually suggested. The purely religious motives of royal policy in this connection were almost always
backed, consciously or unconsciously, by other considerations—especially *economic* ones.

Here we will try to indicate the extent to which economic
factors were involved in the train of events that culminated
in the 1492 order of expulsion, and to show briefly the probable impact on the Spanish economy of this enforced Jewish
exodus.

*   *   *

The events preceding the expulsion from Spain were complicated by the fact that, in contrast to the situation in other Catholic lands, where they had been the sole non-Christian element, ever since the Arab invasions from North Africa in the eighth century the Jews of the Iberian Peninsula had lived side by side with this very important ethnic group, who, economically and socially, eventually found themselves in a position not very different from that of the Jews. The attitude of the dominant class toward the Jewish community during and after the Christian reconquest was greatly influenced by how these Muslim neighbors reacted to their mutual situation.

A second feature that distinguishes the situation in the Pyrenean Peninsula from that elsewhere in the West is that Spanish Jewry was considerably larger than the Jewish communities of either England or France in medieval times. Edward I's edict of expulsion (1290) had sent some fifteen thousand persons across the Channel to mainland Europe; Philip the Fair, in ordering the exclusion of Jews from the kingdom of France (1306), had exiled a community of forty thousand at the most. The complete absence of detailed and reliable statistical data renders demographic assessments for the medieval period extremely hazardous; yet it has been established beyond a reasonable doubt that the Jewish population of Spain at the close of the thirteenth century was at least 250,000, and some intelligent guesses place it as high as twice that one hundred years later.

Third, whereas both clerical and secular edicts in the other lands of the West had obstructed Jews from becoming landowners and the exclusiveness of the guilds had prevented them from entering industry or trade, thereby virtually confining their economic role to moneylending, in late medieval Spain the Jews formed an organic part of the country's economic life in all its branches. (The extent of their influence in this sphere is suggested below.) But in a land that had been torn by racial strife for the greater part of the Middle Ages, the Christian and later the Muslim readiness to submit to the dominant political caste made things more difficult for the Jews; and, unlike their coreligionists in England or France, many of the Spanish Jews were prepared to make all kinds of spiritual concessions in order to maintain their important economic status. By creating a large body of suspect Christians, this circumstance served to intensify anti-Jewish passions on the peninsula.

Nor should it be forgotten that the final expulsion coincided with the culmination of the crusade against the Muslims (the decree was actually signed in the council chamber of the captured Alhambra), as well as with the discovery of vast territories across the Atlantic in the New World. Political consolidation and colonial expansion led to the emergence of a national economic policy based on bullionist and mercantilist tenets which, by and large, were incompatible with the continuation of a tolerant attitude toward the Iberian Jews.

During the early centuries of Arab political and military power in Spain, the Jewish communities—in common with other non-Muslim groups—had enjoyed complete toleration in return for a comparatively small poll tax. They participated in every sphere of economic activity, becoming farmers (in this capacity they introduced new crops and stimulated scientific methods of cultivation), craftsmen, and merchants; they were also extensively employed in the Muslim civil service as revenue controllers and tax collectors. When Cordova lost its predominance at the beginning of the eleventh century and Granada, the new center of Muslim power, proved incapable of holding together the crumbling Spanish caliphate, the resultant Islamic dynastic squabbles led to large-scale Jewish emigration; thereafter, Jewish enterprise tended to become progressively concentrated in the expanding Christian kingdoms of the north.

In somewhat exaggerated terms, J. W. Thompson has written: "From the Saracen conquest of Spain, with the enormous wealth it afforded them, dates the prominence subsequently attained by the Jews in the political and financial affairs of Europe" (James Westphall Thompson, *Economic and Social History of the Middle Ages* [New York, 1928], p. 191). Nonetheless, by the thirteenth century manufacturing in Castile rested largely on the technical skill of Jewish craftsmen, while Jewish traders were handling much of the foreign commerce of the neighboring kingdom of Aragon. Although Jews were compelled to dwell in segregated portions of the towns, few occupational restrictions were enforced, and Jews had become the leading producers of leatherware, the main suppliers of soap and candles, the chief ironmongers and armorers, important dyers of textiles, and holders of a monopoly in the manufacture of Castilian parchment.

Some of these manufactured articles, together with the agricultural and mineral products of Aragon, found their way to the port of Barcelona, from which they would be carried by Jewish seafarers to North African markets. These merchants had gained special concessions in Tunis and Alexandria, and were also active in importing French cloth and some English wool. Besides building up the international commerce of that expanding port, they specialized in exchanging foreign currencies and in providing banking facilities—services that furnished valuable working models for the establishment of the famous municipal bank of Barcelona in 1401.

As the monarchs of the various Christian kingdoms extended their power at the expense of the Muslims, and the servile-feudal institutions gradually disappeared under the impact of the developing urban money economy, the policy of toleration toward the Jews was whittled away. As early as 1328 the Navarre community suffered a series of brutal massacres; throughout the ravages of the Black Death there were

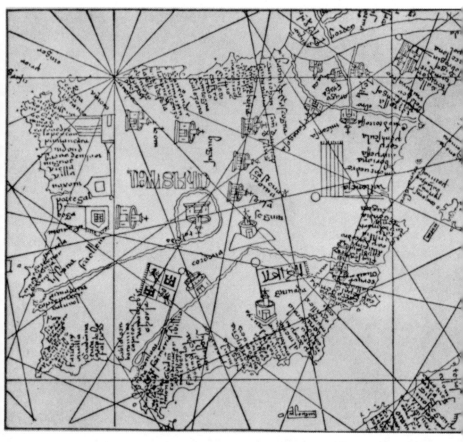

Map of Iberian Peninsula by 14th-century Jewish cartographer

widespread attacks on Jewish lives and property in Catalonia; and during the closing decade of the fourteenth century local outbreaks of anti-Jewish violence were especially virulent in New Castile and Andalusia.

In spite of occasional massacres, growing insecurity, and repressive edicts, the impoverished and numerically reduced Spanish communities slowly recovered from their misfortunes during the early years of the fifteenth century, the most prosperous among them being the "New Christians" or Marranos, who had accepted conversion to avoid persecution; in fact, the stage was soon reached when the leading aristocratic families had Jewish blood coursing through their veins. Nor were the rulers of Spain as yet in a position to dispense completely with the services of Jewish entrepreneurs. In Castile, particularly, they were to be found in key positions as farmers of state revenues, concessionaires of royal mills and salt marshes, financiers of military enterprises, and stewards of crown and manorial estates; in fact, as late as 1491 Ferdinand and Isabella renewed for four years their contracts with some of the prominent Jewish tax farmers.

During this period no law was more frequently reiterated than one prohibiting Jews from acting as stewards of the nobility or as farmers and collectors of the public rents; the repetition of such measures gives some indication of the extent to which financial affairs were still handled by prosperous Jews, who sometimes wielded considerable influence at court. Such individuals, however, were not sufficiently powerful to stem the growing tide of economic anti-Semitism.

According to the available evidence, membership in the Spanish craft guilds was entirely voluntary, at least up to the early part of the fourteenth century. As the central administrations gained more effective power, attempts were made to encourage industrial output by inducing those artisans who were not yet organized to form themselves into guilds; thus in 1336 Pedro IV of Aragon granted a charter to Jewish cobblers throughout his kingdom which permitted them to organize in a single craft fraternity. Gradually, however, nationalism gave way to a much more bigoted racism in matters of guild policy, and by the early years of Ferdinand and Isabella's reign, would-be apprentices had to produce their baptismal certificates and provide full proof of *limpieza de sangre*, or "purity of blood." Through such measures, Jews, as well as Muslims and converts—all of whom had previously enjoyed full access to guild membership—were now virtually excluded from playing any further part in Spanish industrial life.

The power and influence of the Cortes in the conduct of Spanish affairs greatly exceeded that of any other parliamentary assembly in late medieval Europe; important pressure groups of Castilian merchants could make their wishes known and their authority felt there. By the early fifteenth century, although there is some indication that the rulers still desired to obtain maximum economic advantages from their Jewish subjects by making generous concessions to them, pressure from Christian commercial interests was growing in intensity. Every time a monarch met the Cortes, he would receive petitions that begged him to restrict or abolish rights granted to the Jews. Such complaints proved effective weapons of commercial rivalry since they rarely could be completely ignored—the urban mercantile interests that these Cortes spokesmen represented were becoming too important in royal financial affairs for the sovereign to risk giving offense outright.

Besides these industrial and commercial elements, there were also other groups who believed they stood to benefit from the exclusion of Jewish enterprise. As early as 1273 royal recognition of the Castilian sheep-owners' guild of the *Mesta* had been conferred in return for a royal sheep tax; by 1277 this tax was being farmed out to various Jewish bankers in biennial leases at twenty-four thousand maravedis a year, a precedent usually followed by later medieval sovereigns. Enmity had thus been brewing for centuries between these "unbeliever" tax gatherers and the sheep farmers, with the *Mesta* officials losing no opportunity to denounce these "persecutors of Christian shepherds." By the late fifteenth century the organization had reached the height of its influence in royal circles and found itself in a position to strike a decisive blow. In his exhaustive history of the Spanish sheep-owners' guild Julius Klein argues that "there is every reason to believe that Jorge Mexia, the energetic attorney-general of the *Mesta*, who was never far from the royal presence, had not a little to do with the edict for the expulsion of the Jews" (Julius Klein, *The Mesta: A Study in Spanish Economic History, 1273–1836* [Cambridge, Mass., 1920], p. 217).

Economic envy and animosity were also to be found in the broader field of tax collecting and fiscal administration. In the cities, where resentment was mounting against the inherently wasteful and corrupt system of farming out the public revenues, popular prejudice led the public to identify Jews with this practice; the association of Jewish financiers with the proverbially unpopular occupation of moneylending for profit rendered them particularly objectionable. Moreover, many of the feudal nobles, finding it increasingly difficult to make ends meet from the revenues of their estates (owing to the plunging value of their rents) and no longer able to supplement their earnings by going on campaigns against the Muslims (since the wars of reconquest were now drawing to a close), were anxious to get a share of the lucrative business of farming the taxes; they thus had a strong incentive to oust the traditional Jewish revenue collectors.

There can be little doubt, either, that the personal greed of the joint monarchs was an immediately decisive factor leading up to the expulsion and that the establishment of the Holy Office in Spain in 1478 had strong economic motives behind it. As yet the rich silver deposits of Mexico and Peru lay undiscovered, and Ferdinand and Isabella were suffering from a chronic shortage of liquid funds to complete their conquest of Granada, the last surviving Muslim stronghold. Instead, the fanatical Dominican monks—who were anxious to introduce the paraphernalia of the Inquisition—could hold out the prospect of royal appropriation of all or a large part of the Jews' fortunes. In 1481, when the first auto-da-fé was held, the wealth of those Marranos who had been condemned to death or imprisonment went into the royal coffers; even those who had voluntarily confessed *(conversos)* had to pay heavy fines for their "relapse." In 1487, with the final military campaign now imminent, a special war tax was levied on every Jewish family in Castile. Having contributed to the expenses of the fall of Granada out of all proportion to their numbers, they were thereupon expelled. Under the terms of the 1492 edict no gold or silver bullion or coins could be taken out of the country by the exiles. This meant in effect that the refugees were almost completely stripped of their funds; for although in theory they were permitted to accept bills in exchange for specie few genuine opportunities now existed for such transfers, since most of the business in commercial notes had been in Jewish hands.

Thus it seems apparent that urgent financial considerations lay behind the monarchs' acquiescence in the designs of Torquemada and his henchmen. More than one hundred years ago the penetrating (though physically blind) American historian William H. Prescott commented: "It is easy to discern, in this medley of credulity and superstition, the secret envy entertained by the Castilians of the superior skill and industry of their Hebrew brethren, and of the superior riches which these qualities secured to them; and it is impossible not to suspect that the zeal of the most orthodox was considerably sharpened by worldly motives" (William H. Prescott, *History of the Reign of Ferdinand and Isabella*, pt. 1 [1837]).

It was once fashionable among historians to ascribe to the religious expulsions all the economic misfortunes that increasingly beset Spain after the middle of the sixteenth century. Jewish authors, understandably, seldom viewed the issue dispassionately; Graetz, for instance, declared: "By the expulsion of the Jews Spain lost . . . the most active, industrious and educated element of her population, the solid middle-class that not only creates wealth, but sets it in circulation like the blood in an organism. . . . In a word, Spain was making rapid strides toward barbarism as a result of the expulsion of the Jews" (Heinrich Graetz, *Popular History of the Jews*, ed. Alexander Harkavy, 5th ed. [New York, 1937], 4:222–23). This note was echoed by many non-Jewish writers, such as G. F. Abbott: "The Jews went, and the life of Spain went with them. Stately mansions fell into mossy decay, rich cornfields and vineyards were turned into waste land, busy and populous cities were suddenly silenced as by a magician's black art" (G. F. Abbott, *Israel in Europe* [London, 1907], p. 166).

On the other hand, within recent years economic historians have tended to discount this theory; Heaton sums up their attitude with the assertion that "the eviction of Jews and Moors was not a cause of Spanish economic relapse, for it happened too early" (Herbert Heaton, *Economic History of Europe*, rev. ed. [New York, 1948], p. 267), and many of the detailed monographs on the subject ignore the expulsion altogether. Yet no single "cause" ever adequately explains a historical episode, and just as the earlier authors overstressed the significance of the Jewish exodus, so modern economic historians emphasize the impact of masses of American treasure on Spanish commerce and industry, often to the exclusion of everything else. In fact, many forces were at work undermining Spanish prosperity, some of which had their roots back in the Middle Ages; so while the 1492 edict must have exerted some influence on the country's economy, this cannot be gauged precisely.

Certainly increasing persecution during the fifteenth century, if not the expulsion itself, had served to destroy an important industrial class. In 1495—three years after the aggressive drive of the Inquisition had resulted in thousands of skilled artisans leaving the country—King Ferdinand was complaining bitterly at a meeting of the Cortes about the collapse of craft integrity and industrial zeal in the kingdom, as well as the sharp falling off in the industrial vigor of Barcelona, the major manufacturing center on the peninsula. Having for so long relied on the technical aptitudes of Jewish and Moorish craftsmen, the Christian inhabitants of Spain were now unable to fill the vacuum which the expulsions had created. Thus the shortage of skilled labor—a problem that was to increasingly beset Spanish industry—can be linked directly to the 1492 edict.

The shock of the exodus to commercial organization must also have been considerable. Not only had the Jews played an important part in the exchange of commodities, in both internal and external markets, they had also formed the largest group of merchants familiar with foreign exchange operations. Here too, then, was a gap that the native Christians were ill qualified to fill, and the interval between the expulsion and the arrival in the country of the Flemish and Italian satellites of the emperor Charles V (a gap of nearly thirty years) was a period of confusion in Spanish commercial affairs. It was this situation that brought into existence the famous *Consulado* or foreign trade house of Burgos in 1494 —a desperate effort to create an efficient marketing organization for handling the raw material exports of northern Castile, especially the wool from the *Mesta* flocks.

Meanwhile, another typically mercantilist institution, the *Casa de Contratación* (House of Trade), had been set up in Seville to control emigration and trade across the Atlantic. Ferdinand had sent instructions to its officials debarring the sons and grandsons of Jews and *conversos* from participating in colonization activities, but such laws were difficult to enforce, since the Marranos comprised the very class most likely to possess the aptitudes and capital for developing transatlantic commerce and colonial industries. Moreover, relief from these restrictions was a tempting financial expedient for the chronically empty Spanish treasury; as early as 1509 "reconciled" New Christians were permitted, in return for a heavy compensation, to go to the Indies and trade there for the space of two years on each voyage. By the close of the sixteenth century, Marranos—in spite of prohibitive laws— were to be found in Spanish America in increasing numbers. This phenomenon seems to suggest that had the main body of Spanish Jewry been present to participate in the oversea ventures of the Hapsburgs, the economic progress of both colonies and mother country might have been more pronounced.

Since it is never desirable for a productive segment of any population to disappear suddenly, the expulsion turned out to be an unfortunate economic blunder. If the edict of 1492 marked a major turning point in the general history of the Jewish people, it was also an occasion of impoverishment rather than prosperity for Spain.

III

MERCANTILISM

10

AMSTERDAM JEWRY
DURING THE AGE
OF MERCANTILISM

While the Napoleonic era may have witnessed the political and legal liberation of the Jewish communities in Western and Central Europe, it was during the age of mercantilism (seventeenth and eighteenth centuries) that they were gradually emancipated in the sphere of economic activities.

Mercantilist statesmen like Colbert and Cromwell were anxious to encourage the permanent settlement of Jewish immigrants. This, they believed, would not only strengthen their respective countries by introducing new techniques and special skills, but would simultaneously impoverish foreign rivals by depriving them of the equivalent human resources. As a result, by the opening decades of the eighteenth century West European Jewry was playing a role of growing economic importance, and this had come to be widely recognized. Addison, for instance, was declaring in *The Spectator* for September 27, 1712, that "they [the Jews] are so disseminated through all the trading Parts of the World, that they are become the Instruments by which the most distant Nations converse with one another, and by which Mankind are knit together in a general Correspondence. They are like the Pegs and Nails in a Great Building, which though they are but little valued in themselves, are absolutely necessary to keep the whole Frame together."

Paradoxically, however, by far the most influential Jewish community during the age of mercantilism was to be found in a land that scorned mercantilist devices and for the most part followed a policy of economic liberalism.

Near the beginning of his long voluntary exile in Amsterdam, the great French philosopher and scientist Descartes commented in a letter dated May 15, 1631: "In this large city in which I am there is not a single man save myself, who does not occupy himself with merchandise. Everyone is so intent upon his profit that I could live here my whole life without being seen by anyone."

Nor was the Frenchman exaggerating. Amsterdam, as the chief city of the most active trading country in Europe, had become the entrepôt par excellence, the principal emporium for both the European and the colonial trades, as well as the financial hub of the Continent.

Even Baruch Spinoza—the most important man of letters produced by this "New Jerusalem," as it came to be called— was a merchant before his excommunication. To this Dutch metropolis (which enjoyed few natural resources and owed its preeminence as a manufacturing, shipping, and financial center to an extremely favorable trading site), a group of Marranos and an impoverished band of East European Jews were to be attracted and transformed into a flourishing community of international economic importance.

Jewish money changers had been active in Amsterdam as early as the fourteenth century; a hundred years later Jewish traders there were carrying on a lively commerce with their coreligionists on the Iberian Peninsula at a time when the foreign trade of Spain and Portugal was almost exclusively in Muslim and Jewish hands. But the origins of the Amsterdam community must be sought mainly in the transfer of economic power northwards from Antwerp during the Dutch struggle for independence.

The Treaty of Utrecht (1579) was followed by mounting religious intolerance in the southern Netherlands toward non-Catholics; the result was a general emigration, with many of the refugees making their way to the textile-manufacturing towns of Leiden and Haarlem; most of the Marranos of Antwerp, however, turned their faces toward the city on the Amstel.

It should not be imagined that the Amsterdam authorities were moved mainly by humanitarian considerations when they permitted Marrano settlement and, later, freedom of Jewish worship. For the most part they were prompted to take these steps for economic motives: it was well known that the fugitives retained important commercial connections with foreign markets, that they had special aptitudes for trade, and that they commanded a certain amount of metallic wealth. Moreover, there was a widespread conviction in the young republic that commercial development was only possible through the periodic infusion of "new blood."

Pieter de la Court, a Dutch political economist, writing in 1662, insisted, for example, that "next to the freedom to worship God comes freedom to make one's living for all inhabitants. Here [in Amsterdam] it is very necessary to attract foreigners. And although this is of disadvantage to some old residents who would like to keep the best solely for themselves and pretend that a citizen should have preferences above a stranger, the truth of the matter is that a state which is not self-sufficient must constantly draw new inhabitants to it or perish" (Pieter de la Court, *Interest van Holland ofte Gronden van Holland-Welvaren* [Amsterdam, 1662], p. 38).

It is not surprising, therefore, that when Henry IV of France told the ambassador of the United Provinces that the favorable treatment of Jews was "an indecent thing for

Christians to do," he received the following classic reply: "Since God could have destroyed the Jews, and did not, this was an indication that He wished these people tolerated on earth, and since they had to be somewhere, it could not be godless to permit them to live in Amsterdam."

By the opening decade of the seventeenth century the Holy Office was becoming increasingly hostile toward "New Christians," and a direct flow of Marrano immigration from Portugal was under way.

In 1630 the Sephardic community of Amsterdam numbered about 1,000 (out of a total estimated population of 115,000). In the middle of the century Ashkenazic Jews—German refugees from the ravages of the Thirty Years' War and Polish fugitives from the Chmielnicki persecutions—began arriving in Amsterdam in increasing numbers. Thus by the close of the seventeenth century the Jewish community had topped 10,000 and constituted more than 5 percent of the total population; by this time Jews were playing an active part in the city's teeming economic life.

It was only to be expected that Jewish participation in the industries and crafts of Amsterdam would, in the main, be directed to new types of enterprise where there were no established vested interests (such as guilds) to hamper progress.

The development of direct commercial contacts between Holland and the Far East had led to the importation of considerable quantities of Chinese raw silk, on the basis of which the Marrano community built up a flourishing silk industry in Amsterdam. Trade across the Atlantic brought in large amounts of raw sugar from the West Indies and South America, and here again "Portuguese merchants of the Jewish nation" were soon petitioning the local government for permission to establish sugar refineries.

By the middle of the seventeenth century the Amsterdam sugar industry was employing fixed capital equipment on an extensive scale (refining plants seldom changed hands for less than fifty thousand guilders), one-quarter of the annual taxes on goods weighed in the public warehouses was paid by refiners, and more than one hundred ocean-going vessels were fully employed in the sugar-trading fleet. By that time, too, Jewish sugar dealers were selling the refined product in the Scandinavian and German markets, as well as in England and France.

Another Amsterdam industry established and largely controlled by Jews was diamond cutting. Although the supply of stones was very limited until the Brazilian discoveries in 1728, there are records of Portuguese Jewish diamond polishers in the city as early as 1615. By the middle of the eighteenth century the diamond industry was providing a livelihood for at least six hundred Jewish families, and a contemporary Dutch author noted: "Often they [the Jews] are necessary in the most lucrative transactions. . . . They are especially active in the precious stones business. . . . Many Amsterdam Jews polish precious stones, etc., above all, they work in rough diamonds. A large number of them are exclusively engaged in this endeavor" (Van der Oudermeulen, *Recherche sur le commerce* [Amsterdam, 1778], quoted in M. Wolff, "De Eerste Vestiging der Joden in Amsterdam, hun politieke en economische toestand," *Bijdragen voor Vaderlandsche Geschiedenis en Oudheidkunde* [1913], 1:99).

And in 1748, when three hundred Christian diamond workers petitioned the government to limit Jewish apprenticeship in the industry and to forbid the Jews to work on Sundays, the authorities refused to take action because "the Jews have established the diamond trade in this city."

In January 1627 the first Hebrew book printed in Amsterdam came from the press of Rabbi Menasseh ben Israel. By that time the Dutch printing presses were probably producing more books than all the other countries of Europe together, and in Amsterdam itself thirty thousand workers were earning their living from the book industry. Conditions were ripe for the rise of a great Hebrew press in the city: the Jews of Iberian origin were a highly cultured group and were displaying increasing interest in both religious and secular literature; there was freedom from censorship; the community had extensive commercial contacts with other parts of the world; and, on the negative side, the Venetian Hebrew printing houses were declining.

Within a few decades the Amsterdam Hebrew press was providing almost all of Europe with Hebrew books, some of which had become models of fine printing.

But Jewish participation in book production was by no means confined to Hebrew works; Joseph Athias, for example, remarked in an introduction to a Hebrew-Yiddish Bible of 1687: "For several years I myself printed more than a million Bibles for England and Scotland. There is no plowboy or servant girl there without one." Nor need his word be doubted, since the States-General had presented him with a gold chain for producing "the most correct and exact edition of the Bible that has ever been published."

There was one other industry with which Amsterdam Jewry was actively concerned: tobacco spinning and dressing. Shortly after the introduction of tobacco into Holland (1611), Jews are known to have been active in its manufacture and trade. Their connections with Marranos in Spain placed them in a favorable position to procure supplies from the Spanish American colonies, and by the early eighteenth century more than one-third of the tobacco firms in Amsterdam were Jewish-owned. Most of these concerns maintained their own spinning and dressing plants, where they also prepared snuff for export.

Illustration from Passover Haggadah printed in Amsterdam in 1695

In this, as in the other industries mentioned, the poorer German and Polish Jews generally performed the unskilled tasks, while the more intricate processes were handled by the Sephardim (Iberian Jews), who also, almost invariably, were the workshop owners, employers, and entrepreneurs.

Thus although exact statistical data is hard to come by, there can be little doubt of the prominent part played by Amsterdam Jewry in the city's industrial life during the seventeenth and eighteenth centuries.

Equally significant was its role in international trade. In fact, not since the early Middle Ages had a Jewish community participated so actively and successfully in far-flung commerce. Through their close connections with Jewish trading settlements in other centers, the Jews of Amsterdam were able to feel effectively the pulse of foreign markets and to obtain favorable credit facilities.

Especially close were their commercial relations with the Barbary Coast, their main concern being the arming of Moroccan ships for acts of piracy in the Mediterranean (this would certainly help to explain why Dutch vessels were frequently spared by the Barbary buccaneers).

Amsterdam Jewish merchants were also involved in disposing of the booty that these pirates had captured, occasionally going to bold lengths, as testified to by J. Savary des Bruslons in his *Dictionaire universal de commerce* (1748): "The Jews of Amsterdam are so expert that, after disguising the merchandise by mingling it with other goods, or packing it in another way or re-marking it, they are not afraid to go to certain Portuguese ports and resell the goods there. Very often they even dispose of it to the same merchants from whom the booty was taken."

But they also engaged in much legitimate trade with North Africa, bringing back cargoes of grain, wax, almonds, figs, and cork.

Whatever part the Amsterdam Jews played in this Moroccan commerce, however, flowed largely from the influence of Samuel Pallache (who was said to be the first man to come to Holland as an avowed Jew rather than as a Marrano); as Moroccan ambassador he negotiated a treaty in December 1610 whereby Dutch ships could freely enter Moroccan harbors and Dutch ports were to be open to Barbary vessels.

Contemporary or near-contemporary Dutch writers, like Jan Wagenaar and François Michel Janicon, contend that it was the Jews of Amsterdam who first established Dutch commercial relations with the Levant, employing their coreligionists at Smyrna, Constantinople, and Aleppo as brokers, commission agents, and interpreters.

The Jewish communities of Venice and the free port of Leghorn were also in close commercial contact with their brethren in Amsterdam; in fact, the Amsterdam Jews invested extensively in Venetian municipal bonds, from which they derived handsome returns.

Things were much more difficult in the Hapsburg territories. Even after the Treaty of Munster recognized the independence of the Dutch provinces (1648), confiscations of Jewish-owned cargoes in Spanish ports continued, in spite of strong protests by Dutch consular representatives. As late as 1716 an official of Brussels in the southern Netherlands confiscated the merchandise of a man named Abraham Cohen and his Jewish associates in Amsterdam on the grounds that, as Jews, they had no trading rights.

On the other hand, after Portugal had thrown off the Spanish yoke in 1640, a treaty of friendship with Holland stipulated that all inhabitants of the United Provinces (irrespective of race or religion) could trade with the Portuguese; needless to say, the Amsterdam Sephardim began to pursue an active traffic with their associates in Lisbon.

Throughout the mercantilist era the sea trade between Hamburg and Amsterdam was very important, and a number of Dutch Jewish firms had branch offices in the German port, where they traded in colonial products, handled bills of exchange on an extensive scale, and played a notable part in the establishment of the Bank of Hamburg. The Jews of Amsterdam also had close commercial ties with Emden, Danzig, and Frankfurt and were regular visitors to the Leipzig fairs, trading polished diamonds and other precious stones for Silesian linen and cotton fabrics.

In France, Amsterdam Jewry maintained a flourishing traffic with the Jewish communities of Bayonne and Rouen, and distributed Bordeaux kosher wine throughout the Continent. Part of the English tin export trade was handled by Dutch Jews, and when the Jewish commercial elements in Amsterdam began to feel the crippling effects of the English navigation act of 1651—a law designed to strike a blow at the maritime supremacy of the Netherlands—their anxiety set in motion the well-known train of events that culminated in the tacit readmission of the Jews to London in 1656; thereafter, Jewish settlers from Amsterdam had an important influence on the growing prosperity of the English metropolis.

Since the main industries in which they participated (silken textiles, sugar refining, diamond cutting, and tobacco blending) were dependent on colonial sources of supply, it is not surprising to find the Jews of Amsterdam concerned with Dutch commerce to the Far East and the New World.

Although Amsterdam Jews were relatively inactive as traders in the Indian Ocean (possibly because the Chinese in Java usurped their position as agents and middlemen), their contacts with the Jewish community of Cochin helped to create the Dutch East India Company's great pepper monopoly. The *grootboeken* (ledgers) of the company's Amsterdam chamber indicate that, besides diamonds, Jews were the most important buyers of mastic, canes, nuts, and aguilawood; in the eighteenth century approximately one-quarter of the company's shareholders were Jews, and its ultimate decline brought ruin to many a wealthy Sephardic family.

It is difficult to determine the exact nature of Jewish participation in the activities of the Dutch West India Company, since the relevant archive material has not yet been sufficiently probed. It is known, however, that Amsterdam Jewry contributed more than thirty-six thousand guilders to the company's initial capital and that by 1674 at least one-tenth of the main shareholders bore Jewish names.

During the company's ill-fated Brazilian enterprise (1624–54) Jews from Amsterdam were active as sugar merchants, slave dealers, and tax farmers; after being ousted by the Portuguese many settled in Curacao, from which they carried on a lively contraband business with the Spanish mainland colonists. Others went to Surinam (Dutch Guiana), where they came to own extensive sugar plantations and to employ many thousands of African slaves; in fact, by 1786 the Jews of Surinam formed the majority of the local European population.

A smaller group of Dutch Jewish settlers in New Netherlands established triangular trade relations with their coreligionists in South America and the West Indies, and when the local anti-Semitic governor, Peter Stuyvesant, petitioned the company to exclude further Jewish colonists in 1654, the directors replied that such action "would be unreasonable and improper, especially in view of the big losses which this nation suffered from the conquest of Brazil and in view of the great fortune which they have invested in the company" (quoted in Samuel Oppenheim, "The Early History of the Jews in New York, 1654–1664," *Publications of the American Jewish Historical Society* 18 [1909]: 9–11).

In short, Dutch colonization and transoceanic commerce had opened a new field of activity for Amsterdam Jewry, and wherever conditions were at all favorable these pioneers, through their enterprise, ingenuity, and ramified commercial relations with the mother city, stimulated international trade and acquired much personal wealth.

Amsterdam's financial preeminence stemmed directly from the stabilizing influence of its bank (established in 1609), which warehoused bullion deposits and served as a guarantee against payments being made in depreciated coins.

As early as 1631 there were 89 Sephardic names out of a total of 1,348 names on the bank's books; that is, while only 1 percent of the city's Christian population had accounts with the bank at this time, nearly 9 percent of the Jewish community dealt with it. By 1674, when Amsterdam Jewry made up less than 1.5 percent of the total population, Sephardic names accounted for more than 13 percent of the bank's accounts.

These facts would seem to indicate that Amsterdam Jewry was actively interested in the important specie and bullion trade and in the export of coins specially minted for foreign markets. There can be no doubt that the bank's facilities frequently served the needs of those refugees whose wealth was in danger of confiscation by the Inquisition, and who were thus anxious to transfer their funds to the credit of one of their connections in Amsterdam.

Many of the Marranos from Antwerp had been active on the Bourse, and the techniques perfected there stood them in good stead in the city on the Amstel when the Amsterdam Exchange was set up in 1614.

Four years later a French diplomat living in Amsterdam commented on the nature of the Jewish influence on the Amsterdam Exchange: "They [the Jews] already exert an influence on the stock of the East India Company and are heeded by the city because of their knowledge of foreign news and commerce. In both matters they obtain their information from the other Jewish communities with which they are in close contact. . . . By this means the Jews in Amsterdam are the best informed about foreign commerce and news of all people in the world. They come together on Sundays to discuss the news of the week, when other people are in church. In this way their brokers can spread the news to advantage on the market Monday mornings" (L. Vignols, "Le Commerce hollandais et les Congrégations juives à la fin du XVIIe siècle," *Revue Historique* 44 [1890]: 329ff.).

There is no doubt that Jews did exert influence on the exchange through their international connections with other Jewish communities.

The fact that the Sephardim had a special place on the floor of the exchange for dealings in securities and that they were prominent on the committees to draft rules for the stabilization of speculation further indicates their importance.

It was through the exchange, too, that most of the commercial bills used in local and foreign trade were negotiated; and so important were the Jews in these transactions that in 1753 a contemporary historian drew up a calendar designating the hour of the inception and conclusion of the Sabbath, remarking: "Because of the multiplicity of the transactions [in bills of exchange] with the Jews of Amsterdam and their daily negotiations and commerce, it is necessary for the Christians to know at what time on Fridays the Jewish Sabbath begins and when it ends on Saturdays. We have therefore drawn up this neat schedule of Sabbath times for the entire year" (Isaac LeLong, *De Koophandel van Amsterdam* [Rotterdam, 1753], 1:157).

Since the Bank of Amsterdam limited its activities to the bullion trade and the opening of accounts, there existed tremendous scope for bill dealings on the part of those Jewish merchants who conducted banking business as an integral part of their commercial activities; there were also a few persons who specialized solely in such bill operations.

Because large quantities of the precious metals were always available in Holland, Amsterdam also became a great center for raising international loans. In an environment where moneylending was practiced on a considerable scale, it is not surprising to find the local Jewish community active in this traditional capacity. When the exiled King Charles of England sent an emissary on a fund-raising campaign across Europe in 1656, the latter was instructed to make Amsterdam his first stop to inquire whether the Jews were in a lending mood.

In 1689 Amsterdam Jewry is reported to have lent William III more than 2 million guilders for his campaign in England, while in 1701 the Austrian government dispatched the court treasurer to negotiate a loan from "the Portuguese Jews of Amsterdam," offering the Hungarian copper mines as security.

In view of its varied financial activities, it is not surprising that Amsterdam Jewry produced several notable economic theorists. One was Joseph Felix de la Vega (who also wrote dramas and short stories in Hebrew); in 1688 he published an analysis of the technique of transactions on the stock exchange, with important suggestions for overcoming current frauds and evils. The fact that the book was written in Spanish rather than Dutch suggests that it was mainly designed for Jewish readers beyond the boundaries of Holland.

A century later (1771) a work entitled *Traité de la circulation et du crédit,* by Isaac de Pinto, appeared; de Pinto was born in Amsterdam in 1717 and became a director of both the West and East India Companies, as well as an important international financier. His tract, which has been acclaimed as one of the great documents in the history of political economy, discusses the workings of the option market and shows under what conditions speculators should operate as bears or bulls.

The relative economic decline of Holland during the eighteenth century was brought about by many circumstances.

There were the injuries done to the Dutch carrying trade by the French and English navigation acts. Retaliatory measures by the States-General helped to create the numerous costly commercial wars of the late mercantilist era and saw the introduction of various restrictive policies in Holland itself, at a time when commercial pursuits in most West European territories were becoming comparatively free. Moreover, stagnation in Central Europe (a long-term consequence of the Thirty Years' War) meant that the transit trade along the Dutch rivers to Germany and other interior markets gradually diminished.

To make matters worse, there was growing political instability, caused partly by the tug-of-war between the provinces and the central administration and partly by the struggle between the monarchist and republican factions.

In Amsterdam itself the growing uncertainty produced by these various factors manifested itself in a marked tendency toward speculation of an increasingly risky nature. The 1760s and 1770s witnessed many fly-by-night projects and wildcat schemes, and the exchange became subject to violent fluctuations.

During the crisis of 1763, for instance, many long-established Jewish financial houses were sucked into the whirlpool of failures through unwise speculative trading in bills. And in the panic of 1773, brought on by an unparalleled mania for speculation, many more Jewish firms suffered great losses. A pamphlet circulating at this time mentions "the example of the Portuguese Jews, the entire loss of their real commerce and foreign trade in this country, the total decline of their trade with Portugal and the West, the ruin of their sugar trade, refineries, jewelry trade, diamond-polishing plants, and other types of traffic" (quoted in M. Wolff, op. cit. [1912], 10:368–69).

Although some Jewish firms were not ruined by these crashes and others made successful efforts to rehabilitate themselves, the Sephardim as a group never regained their financial eminence.

On the other hand, the Ashkenazic Jews did not feel the crises as keenly: few among their ranks had been wealthy enough to speculate on the Amsterdam Exchange, and although some had acquired a degree of prosperity from foreign trade, by and large the majority remained petty dealers and small-scale middlemen.

Conditions became worse still when Holland was involved in a fourth war with England (1780–84), and by the time that the Chamber of the Batavian republic conferred full legal and political emancipation upon Dutch Jewry in September 1796, the Amsterdam community as a group had lost most of its economic influence, after having contributed so much to the commercialization of economic life.

11

THE ECONOMIC BACKGROUND
TO THE RESTORATION
OF ENGLISH JEWRY

After the 1290 expulsion Jewish communal life came to an end in England until the middle decades of the seventeenth century; yet this historical vacuum was never absolute, and individual Jewish traders paid fleeting visits to the country throughout the next two hundred years in the company of parties of Italian and Flemish merchants.

When the Marranos of Spain and Portugal (that is, Jews who had been forced by the Inquisition to profess Catholicism outwardly but secretly remained faithful to their own religion) began to seek refuge in Holland (which itself was busy throwing off the Spanish yoke) and in Germany, during the sixteenth and early seventeenth centuries, it was inevitable that some Marrano stragglers would also filter into England. By the time the Cromwellian protectorate was set up a Marrano colony of at least twenty families was settled in London; among its members were several important merchants engaged in foreign trade.

At the head of this crypto-community was Antonio Fernandez Carvajal, who, though born in Portugal about 1590, had spent most of his life in exile, first as a petty trader in the Canary Islands, then as a shipping agent at Rouen, and finally (after arriving in England in 1630) as a leading figure in the international bullion trade. At the beginning of the Cromwellian era he was importing foreign treasure—especially Spanish bars of silver—at the rate of some £100,000 worth per annum in return for a wide variety of English manufactured exports.

Since the Cromwell government differed little from its predecessors in its adherence to orthodox mercantilist economic policies, the activities of Marranos like Carvajal dovetailed admirably with the accepted program of stimulating an outflow of home-produced commodities to secure a favorable balance of trade, and thereby, it was hoped, an abundant inflow of the precious metals. Moreover, the neo-Elizabethan efforts of Cromwell's navy to ease the administration's financial difficulties by seizing the Spanish silver fleets were greatly assisted by the detailed knowledge which this handful of Marrano settlers possessed about the organization of the transatlantic bullion traffic from the Spanish American colonies to the mother country.

The shrewd lord protector was quick to recognize that this Marrano community exercised an economic influence quite out of proportion to its numbers, and in 1650 he authorized the council of state to give Carvajal special facilities for expanding his trading operations, which came to include a government contract for grain and the importation of munitions and gunpowder on an extensive scale. Furthermore, Cromwell appears to have been especially anxious for the formal recognition and enlargement of the Jewish colony in London, where the authorities were experiencing difficulties in collecting the taxes and the leading merchants displayed little enthusiasm in subscribing to government loans. According to one royalist sympathizer who was able to air his opinions freely after the Restoration, Cromwell's objective in readmitting the Jews was to secure their services as farmers of the customs and thereby enhance the public stock of treasure.

At the same time, as already noted, England's mid-seventeenth century mercantilist statesmen, like their counterparts in Louis XIV's France, were extremely eager to encourage the immigration and permanent settlement of economically useful aliens, with their new techniques and skills—not only a plus for their new homelands but a minus for the countries that had lost their talents.

Such mercantilist reasoning on the positive and negative advantages of state-sponsored immigration helped to place many Jewish communities of Western and Central Europe on a new footing during the seventeenth century. Toward the end of his great synthesis on mercantilism, Eli Heckscher investigated this issue and drew this inference: "In spite of the incidental differences in outlook, which have always existed and will probably always exist where the Jews are concerned, this much is clear, that the leaders of mercantilist policy wished to extend toleration even to the Jews, and that this toleration was determined primarily by commercial considerations" (Eli F. Heckscher, *Mercantilism*, ed. E. F. Söderlund, 2 vols., 2d rev. ed. [New York, 1955], 2:305).

It appears, then, that Cromwell and his advisers were attracted more by the potential economic value of the Jews than by any religious or humanitarian feelings flowing from their Puritan outlook on life. Werner Sombart, who has been accused on the one hand of being an "intellectual anti-Semite," and on the other hand of grossly exaggerating the Jewish influence on the development of modern capitalism, does not seem to be overstating the case in this particular instance when he categorically asserts that "in England the Jews found a protector in Cromwell, who was actuated solely by considerations of an economic nature. He believed that he would need the wealthy Jewish merchants to extend the financial and commercial prosperity of the country. Nor was he blind to the usefulness of having moneyed support for the government" (Werner Sombart, *The Jews and Modern Capitalism* [London, 1913], p. 17).

Who were these "wealthy Jewish merchants" whom Cromwell was so interested in? At that time Holland was, of course, England's principal foreign trade rival, and it was mainly against the Dutch that Cromwell's famous navigation act of 1651 had been directed. Nor did it escape the notice of those English pamphleteers who were busily engaged in trying to ferret out the secret of Dutch commercial supremacy that for almost a century Holland, and particularly Amsterdam, had been a haven for Jews migrating northward from the Iberian countries—Jews who had come to play an important role in building up the trading prosperity of the United Provinces. This situation was bound to be commented on in a land then obsessed by envy and admiration of the Dutch.

Until 1651 the Jews of Amsterdam had been able to carry on a profitable trade with the plantations of the West Indies, importing raw sugar to be refined in Holland and exporting both Dutch and English manufactured goods in return. This commercial link had been strengthened after the Portuguese had ousted the Marrano colonists of Pernambuco (in northern Brazil), many of whom had become sugar planters on the English islands. When Amsterdam Jews began to be hurt by the 1651 navigation act, whereby England restricted the use of foreign ships for trade, they naturally became anxious to secure a foothold in London and thus be in a position to continue their transatlantic trading activities within the framework of the act.

It is not without significance, therefore, that when the idealistic Amsterdam rabbi Menasseh ben Israel presented his famous petition to the lord protector seeking the readmission of the Jews to England, he bolstered his religious and humanitarian arguments with commercial considerations: "For thence, I hope, there will follow a great blessing from God upon them, and a very abundant trading unto and from all parts of the World, not only without prejudice to the English Nation, but for their Profit, both in Importation and Exportation of goods" (quoted in Lucien Wolf, *Menasseh ben Israel's Mission to Cromwell* [London, 1901], pp. 78ff.).

The wheel of history had turned a full circle: what had once been an element of economic embarrassment to Edward I had now become to Cromwell a means of transplanting a slice of Dutch prosperity to English soil.

Armed with Rabbi Menasseh's petition, Cromwell summoned a conference to discuss the whole issue of Jewish readmission, with delegates representing church, government, and commercial interests. For almost two weeks during December 1655 the debate, which revolved mainly around the economic aspects of the problem, continued in the chambers of Whitehall. The spokesmen of the powerful chartered companies were especially voluble in their opposition, protesting that the readmission of the Jews would merely serve to enrich aliens at the expense of native traders and English commerce. Ultimately this opposition found expression in a formal proposal that the Jews, if readmitted, be confined to minor provincial ports and not be allowed to engage in overseas trade. In short, it soon became apparent to the lord protector that he would antagonize powerful vested interests if he insisted that the conference pass a formal resolution in favor of Jewish resettlement.

Officially, therefore, the whole question was shelved, and Cromwell seems to have become convinced that some sort of back-door settlement was the only practical course to follow. His opportunity came a few months later, when in

To His Highnesse Oliuer Lord Protector of The Comonwealth of England. Scotland. and Ireland. & the Dominions thereof

Humbly Sheweth — The Humble Petition of The Hebrews at Present Reziding in this citty. of London whose names ar Vnderwritten

That Acknolledging The Manyfold fauours and Protection yor Highnesse hath bin to graunt vs in order that wee may with security meete priuately in our particular hou to our Deuotions, And being desirous to be fauoured more by yor Highnesse, wee pray wit Humbleneswe yt by the best meanes which may be Such Protection may be graunted vs in Writing as that wee may therewith meete at our said priuate deuotions in our Particula houses without feare of Molestation either to our persons familics or estates, our desire being to Liue Peaceably Vnder yor Highnes Gouernement, And being wee ar all mortall wee allsoe Humbly pray yor Highnesse to graunt vs Licence that those which may Dey of our na may be buryed in Such place out of the cittye as wee Shall thinck Conuenient with the Propri leaue in whose land the place Shall be, and soe wee shall as well in our life tyme, as at our be nighly fauoured by yor Highnesse for whose Long Life and Prosperity wee Shall Continually to the Almighty God &c

Menasseh ben Israel

[signatures]

Wee doe referr this Petition
to the Consideration of yor Counsell.

March ye 24
1655/1

Petition to Cromwell

Engraving of Menasseh ben Israel by Salom Italia

March 1656 a formal state of war was declared with Spain. Most of the members of the little Marrano community had been born in Spain and could have been regarded as Spanish subjects, with all their property subject to lawful seizure. A test case followed, in which an affluent Marrano merchant successfully pleaded that he was a refugee Jew who had fled the Spanish Inquisition. In effect, therefore, the law now recognized the existence of Jews in the country without the royal edict of 1290 having ever been repealed.

This was the typical English compromise that Cromwell had hoped for. The whole situation was illogical, but for the Marrano community, now able to proclaim their adherence to Judaism openly, it was an unexpectedly satisfactory working arrangement.

In the general reaction against Puritan rule that followed the restoration of the Stuarts, any formal authorization of Jewish resettlement might have also been swept away; thus during the next hectic decade the Marranos of London had reason to be doubly pleased that Cromwell had connived at a back-door arrangement. Yet even if such an edict had existed it is possible that it might have survived in the new political climate, as the navigation act of 1651 did. The reason is that while he was in exile Charles II himself had not only been approached by the king of Portugal through a Jewish agent in the Low Countries, but had also secured direct financial assistance from Amsterdam Jewry, many of whom were ardent sympathizers with the royalist cause—if only because they were still incensed about Cromwell's anti-Dutch navigation laws. Indeed, while negotiations were in progress over the largest of these loans, Charles had instructed his envoys to promise the Jews of Amsterdam that, once restored to power, he would guarantee their special protection in his dominions. Since both the Cromwellian and the royalist factions had come to recognize its economic benefits, Jewish resettlement was virtually inevitable no matter which party ultimately gained the upper hand in England.

One last piece of evidence provides conclusive proof that the reason for the restoration of English Jewry was essentially economic in character: when the privy council authorized the residence of Jews in England in August 1664, reference was made only to "Jews trading in or about His Majesty's City of London," who were now assured of "the same favour as formerly they have had, so long as they demean themselves peaceably and quietly with due obedience to His Majesty's Laws and without scandal to his Government"; and it was only in 1673 that official steps were taken to define the religious status of English Jewry.

Though many decades were still to elapse before the restored community was fully emancipated and Jews were placed on an equal footing with the king's other subjects, the very act of readmission itself, which resulted in a considerable upswing in the country's Jewish population, had an important though not easily calculable influence on the economic progress of late seventeenth-century England. Certainly it played a significant part in the gradual transfer of European financial leadership from Amsterdam to London.

12

THE JEWS
IN EARLY BRITISH
ECONOMIC THOUGHT

It is instructive to speculate briefly on the vacillating attitudes adopted toward the Jews by British economists during the century or so that followed readmission, since that era of Jewish consolidation coincided with the vital formative period of classical economics which was to culminate in the appearance of Adam Smith's masterly synthesis, *The Wealth of Nations,* in 1776.

Dispassionate inquiries into economic problems were few and far between before the middle decades of the seventeenth century. There had been, of course, a growing spate of pamphlets on a host of topics ever since the appearance of the printing press in England, but the bulk of these writings were special pleadings in behalf of particular vested interests. Specific references to Jews on the contemporary scene are rare in these early tracts, but they do contain frequent biblical allusions to the economic activities of the ancient Israelites in order to bolster or refute diverse arguments.

Although the playwrights of the Elizabethan Age (especially Marlowe in *The Jew of Malta* and Shakespeare in *The Merchant of Venice*) had propagated the concept of the Jew as a ruthless type of moneylender, the utopian philosopher-economists of the seventeenth century adopted a much more enlightened view. Sir Francis Bacon, for instance, in his post-humously published outline of an ideal commonwealth, *The New Atlantis* (1627), places Jews as well as Christians on his imaginary island, allows them religious freedom, and puts some of his most important views into the mouth of Joabin, a Jewish merchant. And in the very year (1656) when the behind-the-scenes negotiations were proceeding between Menasseh ben Israel and Cromwell's government for the readmission of the Jews, James Harrington, in his *Common-wealth of Oceana,* gave a realistic and sympathetic account of traditional Jewish moneylending activities and suggested that a good cure for the economic ills of Ireland would be to colonize it with Jews, who should be invited to make it their promised land and be given complete freedom to practice their customs and to own property.

The *New Atlantis* inspired the organization in 1645 of the Invisible College for the discussion of natural philosophy, out of which the Royal Society grew. The founding of the Royal Society in 1662 was to exercise a profound influence on English scholarship and letters, and in the sphere of economics it encouraged a tendency to subject economic phenomena to scientific methods of inquiry. One of the most influential of the new school of writers was Sir William Petty, whose many and varied economic tracts served as a much-needed antidote to some of the orthodox mercantilist views of his predecessors. Petty severely criticized many traditional English prejudices, as became a man of the world who had traveled extensively abroad, yet he could not bring himself to adopt an objective standard toward the Jews; although he acknowledged their importance in Dutch commerce and in the trade of the Turkish Empire, he went on in his *Treatise of Taxes*

(1662) to assert: "As for Jews, they may well bear somewhat extraordinary, because they . . . hold it no disparagement to live frugally, and even sordidly among themselves, by which way alone they become able to under-sell any other Traders, to elude the Excise . . . as also other Duties, by dealing so much in Bills of Exchange, Jewels and Money, and by practising of several frauds with more impunity than others; for by their being at home every where, and yet no where they become responsible almost for nothing" (*Economic Writings of Sir William Petty*, ed. C. H. Hull, 2 vols. [Cambridge, 1899], 1:84). Having thus thrown in his sympathies with those commercial elements who had been opposed to the readmission of Jews by the lord protector, Petty then made some curious suggestions on the desirability of subjecting recent Jewish immigrants to a strict discipline and to higher levies.

In contrast to these biased views of Petty's, the closing decades of the seventeenth century witnessed a more favorable attitude on the part of many writers, coupled with a widespread recognition of the Jews' potential importance to the expanding English economy. At this time one of the main concerns of pamphleteers was why and how the Dutch were able to conduct such a flourishing foreign trade, and in his *Observations upon the United Provinces* (1672) Sir William Temple suggested that religious tolerance and freedom might be one possible reason, mentioning in particular that "the Jews have their allowed synagogues in Amsterdam and Rotterdam." In 1680 the anonymous author of *Britannia Languens, or a Discourse of Trade* expressed concern that, while Jews in England "cannot buy a house," the French were "angling" for them, with Louis XIV offering the prosperous Leghorn community all sorts of inducements to settle in Marseilles; the removal of civil disabilities on the Jews, this writer added, would be in the economic interest of the whole nation. The revocation of the Edict of Nantes five years later

led the Protestant countries to hold out many special inducements to attract skilled Huguenot merchants and craftsmen;
in England Charles Davenant—who believed that national
welfare depended upon an active policy stimulating an increase of population—went a step further by suggesting that
the country become "a general Azilum" for all economically
useful aliens, singling out the Jews specifically.

Unprecedented attention was given to the position of the
Jews in English commerce by Sir Josiah Child, chairman of
the East India Company and one of the wealthiest London
businessmen, in his widely read *New Discourse of Trade*
(1690). In the chapter "Concerning Naturalization" Child
summarizes the prevailing unfavorable opinions that (1) "the
Jews are a subtil People, prying into all kinds of Trades, and
thereby depriving the English Merchant of that profit he
would otherwise gain"; (2) "they are a penurious People,
living miserably," and therefore can afford to undercut their
commercial rivals; (3) "they bring no Estates with them, but
set up with their Pens and Ink only; and if after some few
Years they thrive and grow rich, they carry away their Riches
with them to some other Country . . . which is a publick loss
to this Kingdom."

Refusing to accept such racial bigotry, Child refutes these
assertions in no uncertain terms: the more avenues of trade
open to the Jews, "the better it is for the Kingdom in general," while there is "nothing in the World more conducing
to enrich a Kingdom than thriftiness"; moreover, he denies
the allegation that "they bring over nothing with them," and
suggests that if they are given "the same freedom and
Security here as they have in Holland" they will become
even more economically useful and have no incentive to quit
England.

Child's vindication of Jewish commercial activities must

have exerted a profound influence on his successors, for the scattered references to Jews in the economic literature of the early eighteenth century are insignificant and mainly color-less. Even that most energetic of controversialists, Daniel Defoe (whose pen seldom ran dry on miscellaneous economic topics), had nothing to say—favorable or unfavorable —about those Jews who were increasingly engaged in bank-ing, stock-exchange, and foreign trade operations, except to remark in his *Tour of the Whole Island of Great Britain* (1727) that wealthier Jews were yielding to the charms of the English countryside and were acquiring residences in the semirural districts around London.

In 1744, however, the attentions of economic pam-phleteers were once more sharply drawn to the "Jewish question." Trade to the eastern Mediterranean was one of the few channels of commerce still controlled by a privileged chartered body, the Levant Company, and a bill had been introduced to enlarge the company's membership in the in-terests of freer trade. Although passed by the lower house, after a lengthy debate the bill was thrown out by the House of Lords on the grounds that any reorganization would make it possible to admit Jews into membership. The defenders of the status quo pointed out that Jews in the Near East already farmed the taxes for the Turks and served as "universal brokers, as well for small as great things"; if English Jews secured entry into the Levant Company, they and their Levantine coreligionists would soon squeeze out Christian merchants altogether. Eventually, the company was forced to yield to free trade pressure, and an act of 1753 abolished the qualifications that had required members to be freemen of London (this had always effectively debarred Jews from joining the company, since existing city bylaws made it im-possible for Jews to enjoy full freedom). But although all subjects were now eligible for admission, there was an echo of former fears in the clause that prohibited Jewish members of the company from employing fellow Jews as agents in the Levant.

In the same year (1753) the old controversy over naturalization came to a head with the passage of the "Jew Bill," enabling Jews to be naturalized under certain conditions (without receiving the Sacrament) upon application to Parliament. Since the expense of private-bill legislation was very great and only well-to-do persons could possibly take advantage of the act, it would seem that the measure was mainly aimed at inducing wealthy foreign—especially Dutch—Jews to take up permanent residence in England. Yet the bill encountered strong opposition, and numerous pamphlets were soon in circulation inveighing against the proposal on both religious and economic grounds and spreading misunderstanding of its real intent. So strong was the clamor of popular bigotry that the government repealed the measure before a single Jew had applied for naturalization.

Nevertheless, an interesting literary by-product of this abortive act were two *Letters to a Friend concerning Naturalizations* by Josiah Tucker, one of the most logical and vigorous economic theorists of the mid-eighteenth century, who was keenly interested in dispelling misunderstanding. He argued that a liberal naturalization policy was one of the most effective means of increasing national wealth, for "is not that country wealthiest which has the most labour?" After the repeal he remarked in his *Discourse of Commerce and Taxes* (1755) that "the thing to be done is to enact such laws as shall remove all the difficulties which foreigners now labour under, without naming the *scare-crow* word *Naturalization!*" Ironically he added: "Such is the force of a proper title, that if the late *Jew Bill* had been called, *A Bill to prevent the Jews from profaning the Christian Sacraments* instead of *A Bill to enable the Parliament to naturalize Foreign Jews,*

all would have been well; and the zeal for Old England! and
Christianity for ever! would have still been asleep."

But such was popular hysteria—artificially engendered by
the parliamentary Opposition, since an election was pending
—that one of the few scenes that can be reconstructed from
the very fragmentary record of Tucker's life is that of a Bris-
tol street mob burning his effigy because he had ventured to
combat public prejudice against the Jews.

This mid-century agitation had no long-term conse-
quences of any significance and certainly did not hinder the
growing Jewish community from playing an increasingly active part in the country's economic life (although nearly
three-quarters of a century was to elapse before the obstacles
to the naturalization of foreign-born Jews were finally swept
away).

Meanwhile the most important contributions to the further development of economic theory were being made
north of the Tweed, where scholars like Francis Hutcheson
and David Hume were busy laying the foundations upon
which Adam Smith was to build so skillfully. These economists of the Scottish school wrote little or nothing about Jews,
although in the course of his visits to France, Hume became
closely acquainted with Isaac de Pinto (author of the *Traité
de la circulation et du crédit*, mentioned earlier) and in 1764
was largely instrumental in securing for him an annuity from
the English East India Company in recognition of de Pinto's
services during the negotiations surrounding the Treaty of
Paris. It was mainly from de Pinto that Hume became fully
aware of the "manifold persecutions which the unhappy
Jews, in several ages, have suffered from the misguided zeal
of the Christians."

There are no specific references to the Jews in *The Wealth
of Nations*, although Adam Smith does remark that a knowl-

David Ricardo (1772–1823), British Jewish economist

edge of Hebrew can be a useful appendage to a university education. In the first edition of his *Theory of Moral Sentiments*, however, he includes a lengthy passage on the Hebraic sense of sin, which he contrasts with the Greek concept of vice. Of more immediate relevance, Adam Smith's *Lectures* (posthumously published) contain a short but accurate observation on the commercial role of the Jews during the Middle Ages, as well as an explanation for the origins of this function: "The only persons in those days who made any money by trade were the Jews, who, as they were considered as vagabonds, had no liberty of purchasing lands, and had no other way to dispose of themselves but by becoming merchants."

Throughout their works, these Scottish economists of the eighteenth century displayed an enlightened tolerance that was often in direct contrast to the chauvinistic writings of many of their contemporaries south of the border.

The opening years of the ninteenth century witnessed a marked occupational redistribution in the ranks of British Jewry, with many of the children and grandchildren of prosperous mercantile families gravitating toward the learned professions. Thus the stage was now set for individual Jews themselves, or those of Jewish parentage and descent (like David Ricardo and Nassau Senior), to start playing an important part in the further progress of British economic thought —a role that they have filled with distinction down to the present day.

13

MERCANTILISM
AND
THE JEWS OF FRANCE

During the Middle Ages the Jews of France had in many ways played a more diverse role in that country's economic life than their coreligionists in England had. Besides carrying out (as the price of toleration) their traditional function of providing the monarchy with much of the liquid funds required for the expensive task of national consolidation, they had also helped to build up great commercial entrepôts (like the fairs of Champagne), introduce improved credit and banking techniques, and expand French maritime trade with the Mediterranean from the inland port of Montpellier. By the time of the outbreak of the Hundred Years' War, however, the Jews of France—in common with other "unnational" elements, like the Knights Templar and the Lombard bankers—had outlived their economic usefulness to the crown, and at the close of the fourteenth century, after wholesale imprisonments and mass expulsions, organized Jewish communal life in medieval France had disappeared.

The rise of centrally governed national states in Western Europe coincided with the emergence of mercantilism, whose advocates stressed treasure as the basic element of economic power and strove to increase national reserves of the precious metals by every possible means.

Such policies could not fail to affect the status of the Jews. It was no mere whim or accident that led the Spaniards and Portuguese to dispense with Jewish services at the beginning of the mercantilist era; controlling vast colonies with rich mineral resources, the Iberian peoples believed that they had found the fount of perpetual prosperity. On the other hand, the Dutch, the English, and the French needed to acquire treasure by indirect means—that is, by fostering manufacturing industries to increase exports and curtail imports. The resultant intense rivalry to gain foreign markets and arrive at domestic self-sufficiency led to a constant striving for large populations, in which every immigrant worker became a potential frontline fighter in this "war" for gold and silver. To the mercantilist statesmen of Holland, England, and France, therefore, even the Jews were welcome and were offered limited hospitality. As owners of capital, as skilled artisans and industrial entrepreneurs, and as merchants with commercial contacts and family ties in distant markets, they could well become an important additional source of national economic power.

By the early seventeenth century, it had become apparent that the transatlantic silver flotillas of Spain and the Portuguese spice fleets were failing to replenish the national treasuries, whereas the northern states were making rapid strides in their solid programs of industrial and trade expansion. Irreparable harm had already been done when the Iberian rulers started issuing decrees forbidding further Marrano emigration. In any case, such laws seldom succeeded in preventing the flight of these "New Christians" with their fortunes—especially when an auto-da-fé threatened. This Marrano dispersion was possibly as important in fermenting capitalist enterprise and economic progress during the age of mercantilism as the parallel migratory movements of Huguenots and Puritans.

Part of the stream was directed to the seaports of southern France, notably Marseilles, Bordeaux, and Bayonne. The influx continued for many decades without interference as long as the immigrants continued to call themselves Christians. In France, however, there was no vigilant supervision of their conduct, and there they began to revert more and more openly to their ancestral faith and social traditions. By the close of the seventeenth century the official appellation of "New Christian" had become an empty formality, and an organized communal pattern had reemerged with scarcely any disguises.

It is no easy matter to reconstruct, even in very general terms, the nature and scope of Jewish economic life in France during this mercantilist era. As manufacturers they were concerned with the textile and iron industries, with tobacco blending, printing, and numerous petty crafts, but seldom rose to positions of prominence in this sphere because of the many restrictions imposed on their activities by the guilds. Some Marranos became money changers and bankers and, in a few exceptional instances, even tax farmers.

It was in foreign trade, however, that the majority carved a special niche for themselves. In general, the articles handled were destined for mass consumption, in contrast with the much narrower traffic in luxuries conducted by the Jews of France during the Middle Ages. Certainly one immediate consequence of the Marrano immigration was increased commerce across the Mediterranean to North Africa: the Jews of Marseilles and lower Languedoc had soon established regular contacts with their counterparts in Barbary, importing ostrich feathers from Tripoli, oil from Tunis, coral and grain from Algiers, leather and wool from Morocco, and dis-

patching increasing quantities of French textiles in exchange. The central authorities were quick to appreciate the
benefits stemming from the commercial aptitudes of these
traders, and in 1668 Louis XIV extended an offer of protection and privileges to the Jews of the free port of Leghorn to
induce them to move to Marseilles.

At Bordeaux, the Jews, as one French historian puts it, "all
opened up warehouses and shops for the benefit of their
fellow countrymen and sometimes only stayed until they had
made their fortunes" (G. Fagniez, *L' Économie sociale de la
France sous Henri IV, 1589–1610* [Paris, 1897], p. 290). Many
of them, however, took up permanent residence in this city
on the Garonne—for example, the Gradis family, who came
to dominate the transatlantic sugar trade and established
commercial connections with the Jews of London and Amsterdam. The Marranos were also active in the Bordeaux
wine trade, building up an export business in kosher wine
with congregations throughout Europe, and paying their local rabbi four livres per barrel for testifying to its ritual
purity. Local officials were obviously well aware of the Jews'
commercial importance, and when an army of mercenaries
was ravaging the neighborhood of Bordeaux in 1675 and
many of the richer Sephardic families were preparing to
depart, they reported to the city council: "The Portuguese
Jews who occupy whole streets and do considerable business
have asked for their passports. They and those aliens who do
a very large trade are resolved to leave and we are very
much afraid that commerce will cease altogether." A few
years later the district intendant summed up the situation:
"Without them [the Jews] the trade of Bordeaux and of the
whole province would be inevitably ruined."

Most of the commercial contacts of the Bayonne community were with the Iberian Peninsula, but at least one
Jewish merchant in Bayonne was a prominent customer of
the Dutch East India Company, and the records of his

agent in Amsterdam are still extant. Although Marrano traders are known to have been active at Nantes and Nice, Rouen, in the north, was the only other major center of Jewish economic activity at this time; here Jewish brokers were active in international bill-of-exchange dealings and in financing a triangular traffic of goods with Amsterdam and Hamburg.

During the eighteenth century merchants in several French towns reproached their Jewish rivals for selling various articles at unduly low prices and alleged that such goods must be of inferior quality; such agitation led to a number of local expulsions, especially in the decade 1730 to 1740. But they never lost the right to sell at fairs, and some of them (such as the Dalpugets of Bordeaux) were even able to establish a series of branch businesses scattered throughout the country; "since they were more active, more enterprising, and above all more hardworking, they often out-distanced their Christian competitors" (Henri Sée, *Modern Capitalism* [New York, 1928], pp. 96–97). Moreover, the Marranos rendered noteworthy economic services to France during the protracted mercantilist struggle against England in the middle decades of that century.

The views of political economists and official government policies toward these Sephardic settlements varied considerably over a span of time, in accordance with changes in the economic climate. The period of original Marrano settlements (during the latter part of Henry IV's reign) coincided with frantic reconstruction efforts following the holocaust of the Catholic-Protestant civil war. While little was done to prevent all groups in the community from contributing to the restoration of prosperity, xenophobic feelings were running high and a policy of rigid bullionism was being followed in an attempt to conserve stocks of treasure.

Under such circumstances the cosmopolitan ideas of lib-

eral economists, such as Jean Bodin, exercised little influence, and government policy was much under the sway of
Barthélemy de Laffemas, a Huguenot tailor who by 1604 had
become the king's chief economic adviser. Having himself
suffered from religious intolerance, de Laffemas was not
openly hostile toward the Jews as such, but he was generally
suspicious of all alien merchants, who, he believed, grew rich
on fraudulent practices connected with bill dealings and
were draining France of treasure. He advocated that all foreigners be registered and forced to secure permits to carry
on business.

Henry IV himself, however, was much more openly anti-
Semitic; although he had been the main architect of the
Edict of Nantes, by which the Huguenots had secured liberty
of conscience and impartial justice, his previously cited remark to the ambassador of the United Provinces—that the
favorable treatment of Jews by the Dutch was "an indecent
thing for Christians to do"—shows his bigotry.

As the country plunged toward financial bankruptcy and
economic chaos after Henry's assassination (1610) and everyone started searching for a scapegoat, animosity toward the
Jews became really virulent. This trend was clearly reflected
in the writings of the influential Antoine de Montchrétien,
who was obsessed with the idea that foreign merchants in
France were behaving "like a pack of thieving lechers" and
was especially disturbed that there had slipped into the country of late years men who did not rest on Sundays and whose
wives refused to sew representations of human figures into
their embroideries. Hospitality to such people, he insisted,
was rapidly turning France into "a cesspool for other countries."

When the Estates-General was finally summoned in a desperate attempt to reverse a rapidly deteriorating situation,
its deliberations revealed that Montchrétien had found nu-

merous disciples, and one anonymous petitioner went so far as to urge the complete banishment of all Jews from the kingdom. The consequence of all this pressure was a royal edict promulgated on April 23, 1615, ordering all Jews to leave France within thirty days or be put to death. However, since the Marranos were not as yet openly practicing their faith, this measure must have proved something of a dead letter from the start.

During the following two decades mercantilist policy in France—as in England at roughly the same time—grew more realistic: as it increasingly came to be recognized that laws against the export of treasure could not be effectively enforced, the bullionists were gradually discredited; instead, a general policy of encouraging exports and discouraging imports to gain a favorable balance of trade was substituted for the detailed scrutiny of particular trading bargains.

The man mainly responsible for introducing this more liberal phase of mercantilism was Cardinal Richelieu, who took a broad view of the country's economic interests and was anxious to encourage foreign trade by every possible means and to develop untapped natural resources. Although the cardinal was strongly anti-Huguenot in his policies, that was mainly because of the political danger which he believed lurked in Protestant circles. Since the Marranos represented no such danger to the regime, they were left unmolested under circumstances favorable to growing Jewish participation in the country's economic life.

A temporary setback followed Richelieu's death in 1642, when the country was plunged into civil strife and was embroiled in numerous foreign wars, although there is little evidence of any marked slackening in the commercial activities of the Marrano settlements. The threads of a constructive mercantilist policy were once again taken up by Louis XIV's able chief minister, Jean Baptiste Colbert, and during his administration (1661–83) the Jews of France were to find ample scope for their productive energies. It should not be imagined, however, that Colbert ever evinced pro-Jewish sentiments on purely humanitarian grounds; his attitude, as we have observed, was determined primarily by economic considerations. He believed that if the Jews contributed to the strength of the state by useful activities in commerce and manufacturing or by investing their capital, it would be folly to penalize them for their religious beliefs; in any event, by allowing their competence full reign he would be depriving foreign rivals of their skill, ingenuity, and resources.

Colbert was not content with generalities but expressed himself more concretely. In an attempt to promote the entrepôt trade of Marseilles at the expense of the Italian ports, it was he who had urged the king to procure Jewish immigrants from Leghorn. He protected the Marrano merchants of Marseilles despite heavy pressure from local vested interests. In a 1673 letter to the intendant of Aix (the region to which Marseilles belonged), Colbert instructed his subordinate to ignore the complaints of local merchants against the Jews; "whereas [he added] the settlement of the Jews has certainly never been prohibited out of consideration for trade, since where they are the latter usually increases, but solely on the grounds of religion, and whereas in the present case it is purely a question of trade, you shall in no wise hearken to the proposals made to you against the said Jews."

In the French colonies, too, Colbert's policy—maintained by his mercantilist convictions that Jews would ultimately enhance the productivity of these outposts—was extremely liberal for the age. For example, in a letter to de Baas, governor-general of the French West Indies (1671), he ordered that Jewish colonists be given the same privileges as other settlers, including complete freedom of worship. He pointed out that since the Jews had made considerable investments in the islands and had done much to improve export crops, they were to be regarded as useful and permanent members of the community.

After Colbert's death, religious bigotry, war, and disruption of the French economy by onerous taxation and other negative royal policies led to something of a reaction—especially in the colonies, where Colbert's policy was completely reversed by an edict of 1685, which decreed the expulsion of all Jews in the French islands of the New World. Its main result was that the Jewish sugar planters of Cayenne departed for the neighboring Dutch settlement of Surinam.

Yet Colbert's teachings were by no means entirely dissipated. In 1709, for instance, a French intendant expressed the belief that Jews made ideal citizens from a mercantilist point of view and should be favored, because they did not invest their capital in land or other immovable property, and since they possessed neither estates nor government bonds "it must necessarily happen that their money circulates in trade." The neomercantilist writers of the early eighteenth century, such as Montesquieu and Goudar, also pleaded for favorable treatment toward the Jews on economic grounds.

Thereafter, discriminatory policies gradually disappeared: in 1723 the wealthy Marrano communities of Bordeaux, Bayonne, and Marseilles received royal letters patent, legalizing their residence; and in 1730 the designation of "New Christian" was officially dropped. Restrictions on Jews becoming active guild members and master craftsmen were removed in 1767, and in 1784 Louis XVI abolished the humiliating special tolls levied on the Jews of Alsace.

The upshot was that for some time before the 1791 constitution declared all Jews to be equal citizens the Sephardim had, in fact, enjoyed a good deal of economic freedom. It is probably true that whenever and wherever the state controls economic life through the detailed regimentation of individual activities, the Jews are usually worse off than under a system of laissez-faire, yet it would seem that during the age of mercantilism in France, they did derive some advantages from the concentrated power of enlightened despotism. And although French Jewry during these centuries never attained the influence or prosperity of the Jewish communities in Holland or England, it did play some part in the economic development of France under the ancien régime.

IV

SHYLOCK
SOMBART
AND
MARX

14

SHAKESPEARE
AND
THE USURY THEME

No Jewish figure in literature has been more discussed and written about than Shakespeare's Shylock—the only remote rival being Dickens's Fagin. *The Truth about Shylock*, a recent work by Bernard Grebanier, destroys many popular theories about *The Merchant of Venice*, replacing them with some new and surprising interpretations. In fact Professor Grebanier returns to the historical facts on which the play was based in order to reevaluate the personality clashes within the drama, and particularly in order to arrive at a more objective answer to one of the basic questions about the play: How did Elizabethan attitudes toward Jewish moneylenders ("usurers") influence Shakespeare?

For any proper understanding of the Shylock-Antonio clash (and it must be remembered that it is Antonio and not the Jew who is the "merchant of Venice") some knowledge of the moneylending problem as it affected the feudal nobility of the sixteenth century is indispensable. By the time Shakespeare wrote the play (about 1597, just after *A Midsummer-Night's Dream*) the feudal aristocracy of Britain and Western Europe was beginning to feel the full brunt of the century's momentous economic upheavals. No longer was landed property the most desirable form of wealth: rural self-sufficiency based on manorial tenures was a thing of the past, the growth of commerce and towns had created a new class of thrustful, enterprising urban businessmen, and the voyages of discovery had brought to Europe such un- dreamed of stocks of the precious metals that (when coupled with policies of deliberate monetary debasement on the part of the rulers of the emerging national states) inflation had generated a virtual "price revolution."

Still hampered by traditional modes of land usage and a medieval outlook that frowned on all occupations not related to the soil, the members of this social class were finding it increasingly difficult to readjust their way of life to the steep and continuous rise in prices and to the supremacy of the towns as focal points of economic growth. A minority took to commercial farming with zest, enclosing their estates to raise wool. There were also some enterprising landlords who sup- plemented their income from agriculture by opening coal mines and establishing iron works. Yet they were the excep- tions—the majority of the landed nobility continued in their extravagant ways (in the words of Thomas Wilson, author of the famous *A Discourse upon Usury* [1572]), "wearing gay and costly apparel . . . roystering with many servants more than needed . . . mustering in monstrous great houses," and of course getting themselves more and more into debt.

Confronted by the need to meet the ever-increasing bur- dens of their establishments, stave off creditors, or renew loans, these gentlemen had to have recourse to the profes- sional moneylender. And when one recalls that during the closing decades of the century the ranks of impoverished noblemen included lords like the duke of Norfolk (owing some £7,000), the earl of Leicester (about £50,000), the earl of Huntingdon (more than £20,000), and many others whose heirs and hangers-on frequented the Globe Theatre (and that these figures must be multiplied at least tenfold to convert them into present-day purchasing power), it is hardly surprising that the Elizabethan dramatists devoted so much attention to the question.

Of course, the "usurers" who advanced these sums were not Jews. The Jewish community had been expelled from England in the late thirteenth century, and English Jewry was not to be restored until the time of Cromwell. It is true that a small number of Jewish merchants, in the guise of Florentines or Venetians, periodically visited London in Shakespeare's time, but their concern was wide-ranging trade, not moneylending.

Instead, the lenders were native Englishmen—for the most part scriveners. As notaries who handled the continual mortgaging of land and had an intimate knowledge of business conditions and the land market, the scriveners of the late sixteenth century had tended to become embryo bankers. As one of Thomas Wilson's contemporaries, Philip Stubbs, complained in his *Anatomie of Abuses* (1583): "The scrivener is the instrument whereby the devil worketh the frame of this wicked world of usury, he being rewarded with a good fleece for his labour. For, first, he hath a certain allowance of the arch-devil who owns the money, for helping to rent such for his coin. Secondly, he hath a great deal more usury to himself of him who borroweth the money than he alloweth the owner of the money. And thirdly, he hath not the least part for making the writings between them."

But in spite of such moral condemnation, the moneylending business had been open and lawful since 1571, when an act of Parliament had prescribed 10 percent as the maximum rate of interest. However, so pressing was the constant need for liquid funds that in practice this legal ceiling was usually ignored.

This question of the moral and legal justification for interest—crucial in the transition from medieval feudalism to modern capitalism—was one that was uppermost in the mind of Shakespeare's audience, and Elizabethan drama is permeated with echoes of the controversy. Almost without exception the playwrights condemned professional moneylending and maintained in this respect a conservatively medieval attitude, no doubt because they wished to support the economic interests of their most influential noble patrons.

Thus Marlowe's *Jew of Malta* (1592) and Ben Jonson's *Volpone* (1606), no less than *The Merchant of Venice* and a score of minor dramatic works of that period, present an image of a new economic society where commercial values and an unfamiliar money ethic provide novel standards of behavior, and where cash as an instrument of charity and liberality must bow to the profit-and-loss criteria of Mammon. It was becoming increasingly difficult to uphold the tradition of all men engaging mercifully in generous acts, lending freely, "expecting nothing in return."

Of all late medieval Mediterranean cities, Venice, with its cosmopolitan atmosphere, should have provided a relatively favorable milieu for Jewish merchants. In reality the Jews of Venice were in a peculiar position: they were not classified as citizens (although many of them were permanent residents of several generations' standing), nor were they regarded as foreign merchants, since they had no homeland of their own. Hence, whenever native Venetians felt that the Jews were becoming too prosperous, discriminatory laws were passed to confine them to restricted areas of trade and to subject them to arbitrary exactions. By the close of the sixteenth century moneylending was virtually the only occupation which the authorities permitted the Jews of Venice to carry on. When viewed in historical perspective, Shylock's concern about Antonio's habit of giving interest-free loans is

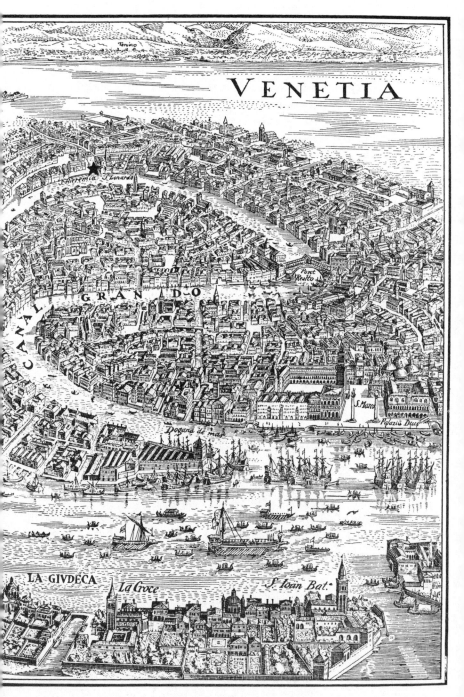

Venice in 1640, showing location of the Ghetto (star)

fully understandable, since it could become a direct threat to his only means of livelihood.

In fact, the basic theme of this clash, this discordant impact of two opposite worlds, runs throughout the play. On the one side we have the merry, spendthrift young gentlemen, Bassanio, "a scholar and a soldier," and his friends Gratiano and Lorenzo. Antonio himself is only nominally a merchant: his business ventures are never in the forefront of the dramatic action, and in manner, conversation, and melancholy disposition he clearly belongs to the world of Portia's Belmont, where money is a means for idle ostentation rather than a source of working capital. Bassanio himself makes no bones about his prodigality: " 'Tis not unknown to you, Antonio,/ How much I have disabled mine estate,/By something showing a more swelling port/Than my faint means would grant continuance:/Nor do I now make moan to be abridged/From such a noble rate." As a prudent way out of his dilemma, Bassanio seeks a loan to cover the expenses of wooing the wealthy Portia.

Antonio's generosity remains unimpaired even when the bond is forfeited. And it is for this reason that Shylock—a product of the new urban cash nexus—hates him: "I hate him for he is a Christian;/But more for that in low simplicity/He lends out money gratis, and brings down/The rate of usance here with us in Venice."

A few lines earlier, the audience is sharply reminded of this clash between the old order and the new: "*Shylock:* Antonio is a good man. *Bassanio:* Have you heard any imputation to the contrary? *Shylock:* Ho, no, no, no, no: my meaning in saying he is a good man is to have you understand me that he is sufficient." Here is a key to the new values that were making themselves felt in Shakespeare's day. The Jewish moneylender is not using "good" or "bad" in any moral sense; the new urban economy, with its systematic methods of double-entry bookkeeping, had made "good" synonymous with "solid financial assets," while "bad" implied a poor commercial risk.

It is not difficult, therefore, to establish that Shakespeare is deeply concerned with the problem of usury in this play. But in view of the fact that England was without a Jewish community at that time, why does he make his moneylender a Jew? No single answer will suffice. In part he was probably exploiting Marlowe's success with a little mild Jew-baiting of his own. As Professor Grebanier argues: "Shakespeare in his Shylock gave the general public enough to satisfy the undiscriminating: if they would have their usurer fairly old and mean to his servants, let Shylock be so. If, despite the fact that the Jews were banished from England and that the majority of usurers must have been Christian, the groundlings would persist in thinking of the usurer as a Jew, let Shylock be a Jew." In short, Shylock symbolized the feeling, shared by Shakespeare, that moneylending was something alien to the national and traditional way of life.

There is, however, another and more subtle reason—one that appears to have escaped Professor Grebanier—which reemphasizes the significance of the usury theme. This is Shakespeare's deft use of dramatic antithesis through pitting a spokesman of what he interpreted as Old Testament attitudes against the New Testament and Aristotelian polemics condemning usury. A close reading of the text soon makes it evident that Antonio's conduct is infused with the spirit and language of the Gospels, whereas the Jewish moneylender emerges as a representative of the Hebrew Bible's apparent legal sanction for the taking of interest from strangers. To rationalize his usurious activities, Shylock draws an analogy between Jacob's methods of increasing his flocks and the "breeding" of money at a rate of interest to augment his own funds: "This was a way to thrive, and he [Jacob] was blest:/ And thrift is blessing, if men steal it not."

Antonio, however, rejects this argument: "This was a venture, sir, that Jacob served for;/A thing not in his power to bring to pass,/But sway'd and fashion'd by the hand of heaven./Was this inserted to make interest good?/Or is your gold and silver ewes and rams?" Antonio obviously allies himself with those New Testament precepts upon which medieval ecclesiastical objections to usury were based—that in terms of true Christian friendship, one lends expecting nothing in return, since "barren metal" cannot "breed" more money.

Of course the distinction between the Torah and New Testament attitudes toward loans was hardly so clear-cut. Originally interest payments were strictly forbidden (Exod. 22:24), lending being regarded purely as a benevolent action, and there was no notion of funds being borrowed for business purposes. But subsequently, as ancient Israel became involved in the transit commerce with Egypt, Arabia, Phoenicia, and the East, the taking of interest was permitted in the case of a foreigner (Deut. 23:20). Luke and the other Gospel compilers, whose audiences were drawn from the depressed, poverty-stricken masses of Roman and Hellenistic society, were not concerned with trading capital or investment funds, and they simply returned to the original Torah stance on the subject.

Ignoring such subtle distinctions and overlaps, Shakespeare is bent on highlighting the clash between the medieval-feudal tradition (with its chivalrous attitude to money) and the new spirit of capitalism; he employs the apparent theological differences between Jewish and Christian dogmas to reinforce his theme—the conflict gathering momentum as the play develops and reaching a climax with the triumph of Christianity in the famous trial scene.

The antagonism between Antonio and Shylock, then, is generated by much more than personal antipathy or even hatred between Christian and Jew. A great deal has been written about Shakespeare's intention in *The Merchant of*

Venice, with one school arguing that the play is simply "a pretty piece of Jew-baiting" and another suggesting that Shakespeare was really defending Judaism and that he intended Shylock to be the sole sympathetic character in the comedy.

But in *The Truth about Shylock* a good deal of evidence is mustered to suggest that the Jewish aspect of the drama is a purely secondary consideration, and that the grand theme of the play concerns itself with the totally irreconcilable values of medieval feudalism and modern capitalism, with Antonio representing the former and Shylock the latter, and the author himself coming down heavily in favor of the traditional as opposed to the new. Shakespeare is idealizing and defending the element of medieval morality that loans ought to be a pure act of Christian charity, without interest. This theme is never lost sight of, and Shakespeare repeatedly takes care to remind his audience of the fundamental conflict between Antonio and Shylock. "Let him look to his bond," the Jewish moneylender exclaims; "he was wont to call me usurer; let him look to his bond: he was wont to lend money for a Christian courtesy; let him look to his bond." When Antonio is rescued by Portia (whom he has never seen before), the mistress of Belmont instinctively acts out of a blind sense of self-sacrifice and class loyalty. So the play ends with the triumph of these idealized traditional values of medieval morality and feudal aristocracy.

At the same time Shakespeare is sufficiently a realist to recognize that the old outlook is doomed. Just before the trial, Salarino tries to comfort Antonio with the remark that the duke of Venice will never allow the bond to stand, particularly since Shylock is an alien. Antonio himself, however, is unconvinced: money and commercial law now form the essence of legal procedure: "The duke cannot deny the course of law:/For the commodity that strangers have/With us in Venice, if it be denied,/'Twill much impeach the justice of the state;/Since that the trade and profit of the city/Consisteth of all nations." True, Shakespeare here is ostensibly writing about Venice, one of the most cosmopolitan cities of Europe; but the Italian setting of the play in many respects is merely nominal, and what was true of Venice was becoming increasingly true of London itself.

The mass of criticism on *The Merchant of Venice* has produced volumes of convincing arguments advocating interpretations of the play so diverse that one often wonders if their authors are really dealing with the same text. Professor Grebanier has performed a service in demonstrating that Shakespeare's Venice is a society caught up in the momentous economic upheavals of the late sixteenth century and standing in grave danger of infection by the inroads of the new capitalistic spirit. The basic premises of medieval feudal morality are being challenged by mercantilism, and it is the figure of Shylock who epitomizes this threat; he is the symbol of the new money ethic in action. Hence to read the play as a vulgar piece of anti-Semitic propaganda, on the one hand, or to sentimentalize the Jew and interpret *The Merchant of Venice* as a clever satire on Christian hypocrisy, on the other, is to overlook the underlying usury motif and to misconceive Shylock's dramatic function.

15

SOMBART
MODERN CAPITALISM
AND JEWISH ENTERPRISE

"Capitalism" is one of those unfortunate terms (like "liberalism" or "estheticism") that can be made to mean anything you wish them to mean. To the economist capitalism is a method of producing goods by means of capital equipment; to the political scientist it is a system of economic organization based on private ownership; to the communist it is a device for exploiting the downtrodden proletariat; and to some historians it represents a particular period in the emergence of Western civilization. When you happen to be an economist, a socialist, and a historian all rolled into one, like Werner Sombart was, your use of the term is apt to become very controversial indeed.

Reviewing certain monographs in a non-Jewish academic journal some years ago, Cecil Roth pointed out that in the past the study of Jewish economic history was largely a hit-or-miss matter. According to the prevailing climate of pro- or anti-Semitism, "it was argued whether offensively or defensively that the Jewish role in economic development had been all-embracing, or that after all it was insignificant" (Cecil Roth, "The Economic History of the Jews," *Economic History Review*, 2d ser., vol. 14 [August 1961], pp. 131–35).

Sombart's *Jews and Modern Capitalism*, one of the most influential books in the field, does not easily fall into either of these neat categories. Werner Sombart was born in 1863 near Magdeburg. His socialist sympathies became known early and acquired for him a considerable reputation, but it seems likely that this retarded his academic advancement, for it was only in 1917 that he gained a chair in economics, at the University of Berlin. Meanwhile, the first edition of his magnum opus, *Der Moderne Kapitalismus* had been published in 1902. This work was subjected to such severe criticism that Sombart began a thoroughgoing revision. To this end he undertook a series of detailed special studies, including *Die Juden und das Wirtschaftsleben* (1911), and *Luxus und Kapitalismus* and *Krieg und Kapitalismus*, both of which appeared in 1912. The fruits of these studies plus a vast amount of additional material formed the basis of the second edition of *Der Moderne Kapitalismus* (1916–27). Meanwhile, Sombart's views on socialism underwent a profound change during the twenties; he had been an ardent Marxist but by 1934, with the publication of *Deutscher Sozialismus*, he had pledged his support to the Nazi regime. Until his death in May 1941 his prolific pen continued to be active.

In short, Sombart's study of the Jewish role in the emergence of modern economic life was one of a series of preparatory studies for the revision of his principal work; and it was written when the author was still very much under the influence of Marxist ideas—long before he had given his allegiance to the official anti-Semitic policy of the Third Reich.

To those accustomed to the traditions of Anglo-American scholarship, Sombart's work presents very considerable difficulties. Not only does he follow in the footsteps of Marx and adopt a negative attitude toward the great bulk of classical economic writings, but his approach is a synthesis of economic history and economic theory.

Early capitalism, argued Sombart, was a unique historical phenomenon that characterized the development of Western civilization between the late fifteenth and the eighteenth centuries. Although certain conditions had to be fulfilled for the emergence of the capitalistic system (such as the development of the modern state, urbanization, some basic technological advances, the discovery of new sources of the precious metals, and improved methods of keeping business records), to Sombart it is the appearance of a "capitalistic spirit" that is all-important. And his *Jews and Modern Capitalism* develops the argument that it was essentially "the Jewish genius" which revolutionized economic life.

In order to establish this thesis, Sombart first had to demolish Max Weber's argument, which had appeared a few years previously, that Protestantism—especially Calvinism and English Puritanism—had played the key role in generating the ethos or "the spirit of modern capitalism." Weber suggested that these religious movements had inspired the individual adherent to devote his activities to a specialized task or "calling" (serving God in the day-to-day activities of his working life) and had fostered the idea that prosperity in worldly affairs is a sign of grace. Although the Protestant sects differ greatly from one another in theology, according to Weber they all share a very similar ethical orientation in which the wholesome pursuit of economic gain tends to affirm one's status as a member of God's elect.

Max Weber's study of the importance of Puritanism in the emergence of modern capitalism was the springboard for Sombart's consideration of the Jewish role in this development. He argued that Protestant teachings hardly encouraged farsighted and adventurous enterprises and pointed out that Calvinistic writings contained even more frequent condemnations of material wealth than did those of the medieval Scholastics. "It would be a narrow conception of the capitalistic spirit thus to see its various manifestations springing from Puritanism," he wrote.

With a good deal of synoptic generalization, Sombart proceeded to argue that the spirit of early modern capitalism had been nourished by the rational approach of Judaism toward economic problems, particularly the Deuteronomic injunction which permitted a different code for commercial dealings between Jews and non-Jews, especially in the matter of interest. In fact, in this respect Sombart tended both to overstress and to oversimplify "Judaism's rationality."

He was on firmer ground with his argument that the Jews acted as a catalyst in shifting the focal point of European economic life from the Mediterranean to the northwest. The Jewish expulsions from the Iberian Peninsula in the late fifteenth century encouraged the growth of capitalistic techniques in the Low Countries and then in England, for the refugees, through their moneylending activities and financial services to heads of states, their standardizing of credit instruments, their financing of colonial ventures, and their expertise in luxury trading, quickened the whole tempo of international commerce and created the foundations of prosperity for great entrepôts like Antwerp, Amsterdam, Hamburg, and London.

But it was Sombart's contention that the specific Jewish contribution to the emergence of capitalism went beyond influencing commercial techniques, types of industrial organization, and the forms of important financial institutions like the stock exchange. Even more decisive was the Jewish influence on molding "the principles underlying economic life— that which may be termed the modern economic spirit." And he proceeds to describe the static, uncompetitive nature of late medieval economic activities based on narrow monopolies like the guilds and sterile doctrines like "usury" and the "just price": "This was the world the Jews stormed.

At every step they offended against economic principles and the economic order. That seems clear enough from the unanimous complaints of the Christian traders everywhere."

Jewish entrepreneurs, according to Sombart, upset the applecart of conformity and regimentation by lowering prices (through concentrating on smaller profit margins and much larger turnovers), by spreading information about the goods they sold and the services they performed (through the technique of advertising), and by introducing the principle of substitution (through launching a wide range of new standardized articles).

In other words, it was Jewish enterprise that brought the concept of economic rationalism to the fore, whereby "all economic activities should be regulated by the individual alone in the way he thinks best to obtain the most efficient results." By championing the cause of individual liberty in economic activities against the dominant views of the time, the Jews had exerted a decisive influence in the shift from medievalism to a world organized on a totally different basis.

In light of research since Sombart wrote *The Jews and Modern Capitalism,* there can be little doubt that this argument is far too dogmatic. That the Jewish influence was important in the economic transformation of northwestern Europe during those centuries cannot be seriously questioned, but that it was decisive is open to grave doubt.

The evolution of modern capitalism was a highly complex phenomenon in which many relevant factors were at work —the spread of a money economy, the eclipse of feudalism, the emergence of the apparatus of central government, the oceanic discoveries, the Reformation (of which the rise of the "Protestant ethic" was only one aspect), the establishment of the great Marrano communities in northern Europe, and so on. All these forces and many others contributed to the changing pattern and tempo of economic life. Sombart, by singling out the Jewish factor, fell victim to the most common of all diseases afflicting economic historians: a penchant for sweeping—and invalid—generalization.

Ironically, recent studies by Jewish historians have helped to restore a sense of balance in this regard. Salo Baron, for example, in his monumental *Social and Religious History of the Jews,* while retaining the Sombartian label "economic catalyst" to describe the Jewish role in this "era of European expansion," recounts in sober, objective terms how Jewish businessmen, excluded from Western agriculture and gradually ousted from many traditional branches of handicraft, penetrated every other available nook in their quest for profitable opportunities, and soon discovered that their usefulness as suppliers of new sorts of goods and improved credit facilities was their greatest economic asset.

In spite of Werner Sombart's assertions, however, it is much more difficult to prove that the whole course of Western economic civilization would have been radically different without this Jewish influence.

16

MARX'S WRITINGS
AND
JEWISH ENTERPRISE

Of all the writers on socioeconomic issues over the last hundred years, probably none has exerted a more powerful influence than Karl Marx. Authors frequently link Marx's name with Freud's and Einstein's when they wish to emphasize the Jewish intellectual contribution to the shaping of the modern world. Are they justified in doing so? Should the Jewish people continue to be saddled with the author of *Das Kapital* as part of their cultural heritage?

It is true, of course, that Marx was of unblemished ethnic extraction. All the reference books and encyclopedias make a point of the fact that on both his father's and his mother's side he was descended from a long line of rabbis. But his father, a prosperous Rhineland attorney, had himself baptized when young Karl was six, and the boy grew up in a completely non-Jewish atmosphere. (His sister, Luise, however, was to reenter the fold when she married a Dutch Jew, Jan Juta, the couple emigrating to South Africa in 1853, where he founded the bookselling and publishing firm that still bears his name.)

Marx, a prolific author, wrote on almost every topic under the sun, and most of his ideas were not particularly original.

Many were merely restatements or elaborations of views put forward by the earlier nineteenth-century school of utopian socialists, though some of his more enlightened humanitarian ideas stemmed directly (but without any acknowledgment) from the visionary societies outlined by the ancient Hebrew prophets, especially Amos and Hosea. It is in fact dangerously misleading to label Marx the father of socialism when the number of claimants to paternity is so embarrassingly large.

The early socialist movement in Europe, in all its diverse forms, had possessed much of the ideological structure and emotional overtones of a religious faith. Most of its propagandists assumed a state of innocence—usually in the shape of some idyllic pastoral or peasant society—which is then undermined by the emergence of "capitalism"; this catastrophic fall from grace inevitably sets in motion a course of events that culminates ultimately in a confrontation ("Armageddon" was the popular term) between exploiters and exploited and the recapturing of universal happiness in a new utopian socialist paradise.

If such a structure of myth and symbolism was to make its appeal to the masses (among whom illiteracy remained widespread), the socialist theorists had to articulate popular resentment against the mechanized industrial society then rapidly emerging. It was not easy, therefore, to dispense with the popular anti-Semitic stereotype. Complex socioeconomic theories meant little to the unlettered, who remained as avid as ever for a mythological narration of the battle between "the children of light and the children of darkness." And with the Rothschilds dominant on the bourses of five major capitals, the Jew of Western Europe continued to be the concrete embodiment of a ruthless money-based culture and an embryo urban-orientated factory civilization which appeared to have no use for the chivalrous code that, it was believed, had once prevailed in the earlier mythical age of innocence.

It was against this background that Marx took a public stand on what he termed the "Jewish question" *(Die Juden-frage)*. This resulted from an extensive literary controversy sparked by a pamphlet by Bruno Bauer, an early Jewish writer on socialism, entitled "The Capacity of the Present-day Jews and Christians to Become Free" (1843)—which was really a plea for both religious groups to adopt atheism. Marx's response appeared a year later in the *Deutsch-Franz-ösische Jahrbücher.* His essay not only continues the anti-Jewish bias of his socialist predecessors but in parts it approaches the same sort of scurrilous rubbish that Julius Streicher was later to popularize in *Der Stürmer.*

Marx proceeds to widen Bauer's purely theological outlook by seeking out the human essence or earthly basis of Judaism. "Let us consider," he says, "the real Jew: not the *Sabbath Jew,* whom Bauer considers, but the *everyday Jew."* Marx has no feeling for the religion of his forefathers: its divine law he regards as simply an arbitrary regulation of material concerns without reference to the true nature of man; to him the whole secular basis of Judaism is the cult of moneymaking— "Money is the jealous god of Israel, beside which no other god may exist. . . . The bill of exchange is the real god of the Jew."

With activities of the Rothschilds in mind, Marx argues that political emancipation for Jewry is of small importance, since, although Jews may be entirely without rights in even the tiniest of the German states, their "financial power . . . decides the destiny of Europe." Moreover, this Jewish cult of interest and profit has now spread to the New World, where the uncomplicated way of life of the early colonists is being transformed by the Jewish sense of values; in the New England states, for example, Marx alleges that the Jewish vendor, with "his goods and his counter on his back," looks on the world as no more than a stock exchange, and his aim in life is simply to become richer than his neighbor.

Having perceived in Judaism an all-pervading antisocial element, Marx next tries to explain why Judaism represents a particular aspect of what he terms "bourgeois society" or "civil society" (catchphrases that he was to use over and over again in his writings without clear definitions; they appear to have implied nothing more sinister than a market economy based on monetary exchange). Judaism has simply been a vulgar practical application of Christianity, the Jews employing their talmudic laws as a cunning device to gain complete control of economic society. It is through such "Jewish Jesuitism" that the Hebrew God has become secularized and the Jews have attained "universal domination," holding the world in thrall to their "egoistic need and huckstering." Moreover, Judaism has been preserved, not in spite of history, but because of history—from its own entrails bourgeois society ceaselessly engenders the Jew.

In short, Marx's argument in this 1844 essay—based on his peculiar materialist interpretation of history—is that the Jew has always been merely the outgrowth of a society built upon an exchange economy, and that with the ultimate establishment of a socialist order there would be no room for either Jews or Judaism. In the Marxist scheme of things there is no awareness of the positive ethical mainsprings of Judaism and no recognition that a Jewish culture had flourished long before "bourgeois capitalism" had become the basic characteristic of economic life. And so Marx reaches the conclusion that religious freedom for Jews must be accompanied by complete social equality. "The social emancipation of the Jew," he writes, "is the emancipation of society from Judaism." Only through the complete elimination of Judaism itself will it become possible to eradicate the abuses of bourgeois society.

In no subsequent part of Marx's writings is any further attempt made to deal with the "Jewish question." In Volume

1 of *Capital* an inconsequential reference to the capture of Jerusalem by the Roman legions under Titus is the only item remotely concerned with Jews or Judaism; Volume 2 is quite *Judenrein,* and Volume 3 merely contains a fleeting mention of medieval Jewish moneylending activities (chapter 36). Why this loss of interest? *Capital* represents a radical departure from classical economic theory: to Adam Smith, Ricardo, and their disciples, private enterprise had been part of the natural order of things, and they had argued in terms of a close harmony of interest among the various social groups; but to Marx "bourgeois capitalism" was merely a passing phase in the inevitable transition toward communism, and he conceived of economic life in terms of a perpetual conflict between property owners who do little or no physical work and the proletariat who own no property. Surely, then, his earlier thesis about the Jewish fly in the ointment should have remained particularly relevant in this context. Since he had argued so phlegmatically that the disappearance of the Jews as a group was a sine qua non for the demolition of the old socioeconomic order, what induced Marx to refrain from riding this particular hobbyhorse when he came to work out the details for the overthrow of capitalism? It is reasonable and logical to expect a continual emphasis on Jewish economic perfidy to echo through the dreary pages of this almost unreadable work.

We can only guess at the answer, since the voluminous Marx-Engels correspondence throws no further light on the matter. It seems reasonable to assume, however, that consciously or unconsciously Marx had resolved to make a tactical retreat in this regard, partly because to an increasing extent Jews themselves were being attracted by the Marxian gospel (ironically, often becoming more doctrinaire exponents of revolutionary socialism than Marx himself), but probably mainly because by the 1860s it was obvious that the ploy of anti-Semitism was a tool for political reactionaries and no longer a useful aid in creating the right climate for forceful socioeconomic changes.

And so this ponderous, meticulous author, this slow, painstaking German scholar par excellence, this atheist scion of venerable talmudic students spent his closing years in abject poverty, neglecting his family, rummaging among musty official Blue Books in the Reading Room of the British Museum, intent on his self-imposed task of demonstrating that the prevailing economic system should not be taken for granted. Economic laws are not immutable, and once the possibility of change is recognized the old argument that everyone has an interest in insuring that the total product to be shared is maximized falls to the ground; for with such a change, those who hope to gain and those who fear to lose are immediately placed in opposing camps. No longer was it prudent, however, to single out the Jews for a major negative Hegelian role in this scheme of things.

Franz Mehring, one of Marx's biographers, lauds the fact that Karl's father "had attained that humanistic culture which freed him entirely from all Jewish prejudices" and that he was able to hand on this freedom to his children "as a valuable heritage" (Franz Mehring, *Karl Marx: The Story of His Life* [London, 1936], p. 4). Be that as it may, one of Marx's aunts might be permitted to have the last word. This astute woman is supposed to have remarked that had Karl spent a little more effort *making* capital and a little less energy writing about it, things would have turned out rather better both for himself and for the world at large.

V

ESSAYS
IN
BIOGRAPHY

17

THE BROTHERS GOLDSMID

One of the basic themes developed in Sombart's *Jews and Modern Capitalism* was the concept of cosmopolitanism as an ethnic trait leading directly to cosmopolitanism as a financial force. The key to Jewish prosperity, Sombart argued, lay in the widespread dispersion of the Jewish people and their acclimatization in many regions; this, he suggested, had enabled them to develop the foresight, finesse, and speculative maneuverability that are so essential in the fashioning of sensitive financial institutions.

And it was Alfred Marshall's belief that "the English had not originally, and they have not now [1910], that special liking for dealing and bargaining, nor for the more abstract side of financial business, which is found among the Jews" (Alfred Marshall, *Principles of Economics*, 6th ed. (London, 1910), p. 33).

In an earlier chapter it was shown that Cromwell and the Puritans were keenly aware of financial power as a factor in political policy—an awareness that had directly led to the tacit readmission of the Jews to England in the mid-seventeenth century. Later the retinue of Catherine de Braganza, the bride of Charles II, included a number of prominent

Jewish financiers, among them the Da Silva brothers, Amsterdam bankers who were entrusted with the transmission and management of the queen's dowry. Still later in the century the recently settled immigrants assisted the movement against the unconstitutional aspirations of James II, and by the time of the accession of William III the Jews of London had firmly consolidated their position in the economic life of the city.

In the purely financial sphere (as distinct from local trade and foreign commerce), however, the activities of these London Jews were overshadowed completely by the local goldsmith-bankers, and the Jews of this period played little or no part in the evolution of English banking technique. But this was a situation that was destined to change.

Perhaps the most persistent trend in eighteenth-century economic history was the relative decline of Holland as a commercial power and the corresponding ascendance of England; the gradual transfer in the focal point of international financial dealings from Amsterdam to London was symptomatic of this change. There is a marked difference of opinion among historians about the precise nature of the Jewish influence on this process: contemporary writers in both England and Holland possibly overstressed the importance of the Jewish role. More than a century later Joseph Jacobs, the prolific Australian-born historian and folklorist, was emphatic in declaring that if London had become the chief financial center of the world it owed this position in large measure to the Jews. Recent studies have tended to minimize the influence of Dutch Jewish settlers on the rise of the London money market, but the debate continues, since it is a problem which by its very historical nature can never be settled conclusively.

But there has always been general agreement among all schools of thought that Jewish immigrants from the Netherlands during the middle decades of the eighteenth century were mainly responsible for the growth of arbitrage and other legitimate speculative operations on the London exchange, and that Jews participated extensively in the government stock dealing which enabled the British treasury to weather the storm of the lengthy Napoleonic struggle.

Toward the end of the eighteenth century two bill brokers, Benjamin and Abraham Goldsmid, became the largest loan contractors in England. They revolutionized the methods of placing government loans with the public, and they were ultimately regarded as the country's leading financiers— Abraham, in fact, being widely acknowledged as "the king of the stock exchange." Some historians have gone as far as to suggest that, like the Rothschilds of a later era, at the height of their prosperity the Goldsmids were in a position to influence markedly the general course of European history.

As the center of European trade and finance shifted from the Dutch capital to London, more and more Amsterdam Jews were attracted to the English metropolis by the promise of higher returns in the colonial trades and inter-European commerce. Among these new arrivals was Aaron Goldsmid, a prosperous merchant who had emigrated from Holland in the early 1740s; he claimed descent from Rabbi Uri Halevi, the sixteenth-century mystic credited with the power of transmuting the baser metals into gold!

Aaron was no alchemist, but he set up business in London as a dealer in foreign exchange and took his eldest son, George, into partnership about 1773; the second son, Asher, joined the firm of Abraham de Mottos Mocatta, bullion brokers to the Bank of England. Meanwhile, Benjamin, son number three, had been sent to relatives in Amsterdam to gain business experience; after his return, he became an active bill broker and in 1776 took premises in the largely

Jewish quarter of Leman Street, where he was soon joined by the youngest brother, Abraham (b. 1756).

Although the Goldsmids were not members of the predominantly Sephardic group of attorneys and financiers who had come to form the upper crust of the British Jewish community, they experienced few of the physical and social hardships that beset the majority of their coreligionists in late eighteenth-century London. On his death in 1781 Aaron had left the brothers some money, but it was Benjamin's prudent marriage to Jessie Salomons two years later that really set the firm on its feet; the daughter of a wealthy East India merchant, she is said to have been the richest marriageable Jewess in England at the time and to have brought him a dowry of £100,000.

In addition to such acquired wealth, the two brothers had built up a number of useful connections: they were on close terms with Abraham Newland, chief cashier of the Bank of England; they gave advice to many members of the aristocracy on stock exchange matters; in Holland they raised money for the spendthrift Prince of Wales; and William Pitt is said to have placed great value on their judgment. Not long after the Peace of Amiens was signed (March 1802) George III himself—in a lucid moment—and Queen Charlotte honored the family with a visit to Benjamin's estate in the select suburb of Roehampton, a district subsequently dubbed "a banking colony" by Thackeray.

From their offices in Leman Street, Benjamin and Abraham Goldsmid conducted a variety of financial transactions. At first they were predominantly bill brokers, and the author of a pamphlet published in 1821 recalled that some thirty years earlier the firm had discounted bills at 4 percent plus a commission of one-eighth of one percent. Moreover, it became the practice for London bankers with short-term surplus funds to purchase bills from the Goldsmids at current market rates and, if subsequently pressed by their depositor, to discount such bills with the brothers, thereby replenishing their cash reserves. Thus more than twenty years before Richardson, Overene & Co. (traditionally regarded as the pioneer specialist bill brokers on the London money market) were undertaking such dealings in a small way, the Goldsmids were negotiating large-scale bill operations.

In addition to such domestic brokerage activities, the firm maintained close connections with the bourses of Amsterdam and Hamburg, dealing extensively in foreign drafts and remittances. With such wide international connections they were able to play a considerable part in the financing of British overseas trade.

When the outbreak of the revolutionary wars restricted operations in the foreign exchanges and the rise in interest rates that began in 1793 arrested the further development of the bill-discounting business, the Goldsmids turned their attention to the handling of short-term government securities, such as exchequer bills; since these could be freely bought and sold on the stock exchange, the brothers' activities in this direction gave a renewed flexibility to the London money market at a critical period. Between 1797 and 1810 some £400 million worth of exchequer bills were issued, the bulk of which was apparently handled by the Goldsmids. Furthermore, to finance the fleet and its ancillary services special navy bills were issued, and in the short space of eighteen months (October 1800 to March 1802) the firm negotiated £4,300,000 worth of these bills, charging its customary one-eighth of one percent commission. Besides selling these securities to private bankers, merchants, and others, the brothers also acted as government brokers, serving as the main intermediaries between the Bank of England and the treasury; and at the end of each financial year when outstanding exchequer bills were "funded" (that is, converted into fixed loans secured by interest-bearing bonds), Goldsmid & Co. were usually major participants, either on their own account or on behalf of customers.

Since the beginning of specialist billbroking was contemporaneous with the very rapid growth of country banking in England, it seems more than likely (although direct evidence is lacking) that the firm had dealings with business houses in the provinces, thereby helping to link up the new industrial areas of the Midlands and northwest with the London money market.

The brothers' removal in 1792 from their cramped quarters in Leman Street to spacious premises in Capel Court—close to the Royal Exchange and the Bank of England—proved to be a landmark in the firm's history. Thereafter, although the billbroking business was by no means given up, Messrs. B. & A. Goldsmid & Co. increasingly concerned themselves with government loan contracting and speculation in the "funds."

The loosely organized London money market—of which the Goldsmid firm was now such an important segment—was transformed into a much more imposing mechanism by the stimulus of war. "England, untouched by invasion or blockade, undrained until 1808 even of human resources, became a closely-integrated economic organism" (Leland H. Jenks, *The Migration of British Capital* [New York, 1927], p. 16), and investments from Central Europe, Spain, and the Netherlands flowed to London, their owners seeking the security now denied to them at home by the Napoleonic onslaughts. It was this inflow, together with an expanding colonial trade and growing productivity—resulting from the labor-saving innovations of the industrial revolution—which enabled the British to find the means for financing the successive coalitions against the French; between 1793 and 1816 the funded debt increased by more than £765,000,000.

This is not the place to delve into the technicalities of the methods involved in raising such wartime government loans. It is essential to stress, however, that it was a situation that offered plenty of scope for financiers of the Goldsmid caliber —the potential profits were high, but the risks, too, were enormous. The alternation of peace and war inevitably called forth a series of financial crises, during which some firms, still quite solvent, experienced difficulties in obtaining cash to pay their immediate way; temporarily discredited, such enterprises easily slipped into the vortex and went down permanently.

Until 1795 government fund raising had been a source of patronage, with all its attendant abuses. In that year, however, with growing calls on the loan market, Pitt began encouraging rival contractors to bid against one another, in the hope of insuring better terms for the Treasury. Forming a syndicate with other merchant-banking firms, the Goldsmids successfully contracted for the £18 million loan and for a similar amount in 1796.

With rumors of an impending invasion from France, conditions in the London money market rapidly deteriorated during the next twelve months; timid people began to withdraw gold from their banks, and faith in public credit was shrinking fast. As the stock market continued to fall and the Bank of England itself became endangered by the drain of gold, the brothers' initial profits in this sphere had soon changed to considerable losses. The Bank Restriction Act (1797)— which suspended further gold payments—came too late to save some of the leading loan contractors, many of whom had failed by the close of the century. The Goldsmids themselves were able to weather the storm, having been shrewd enough to reduce their holding of government stock before the price fall became too marked—in fact, they emerged from the crisis with an estimated capital of £800,000.

Between 1801 and 1806 the firm's role in loan contracting, though spasmodic, remained significant. In 1806 Benjamin, who had always been subject to occasional bouts of depression, committed suicide during a painful attack of gout. Forced to reorganize, Abraham took in Benjamin's brother-in-law, Nathan Salomons, to handle operations on the exchange, and with the assistance of another junior partner he himself continued to devote his own energies to government loans. In 1809 subscriptions to a fresh issue of £14,600,000 were negotiated by the firm singlehandedly.

In the following year, however, a fresh crisis—even more far-reaching than that of 1797—swept the money market, caused partly by the increased severity of Napoleon's "continental system" (the name given his plan to paralyze Great Britain through the boycott of her commerce) and partly by the inevitable reaction to an overexpansion of credit in London itself. Abraham had just arranged a new loan for the Treasury, retaining a relatively small amount of it on his own account. As the uncertainty gathered momentum the new bonds fell from a premium of 2 percent to a discount of 6.5 percent. Temporarily short of liquid funds and unable to meet a commitment of £350,000 due the East India Company, he followed his brother's tragic example and shot himself at his house at Morden on September 28, 1810.

The news of Abraham's death converted crisis into panic: Spencer Percival, the prime minister, rushed back to London from his country house to confer with the governor of the Bank of England and high Treasury officials; special messengers were dispatched to the king and the Prince of Wales; all was confusion on the exchanges. A day later the new loan was selling at 10¼ percent discount. For winding-up purposes the junior partners continued in management, subject to a government-appointed committee of inspection. By 1820, when the doors of Goldsmid & Co. closed for good, 17s.6d. on the pound had been paid, and Parliament sanctioned a bill to release the firm from its comparatively small outstanding debt.

This sudden eclipse was hardly self-inflicted: like many others, the Goldsmids had fallen victims to the vagaries of wartime financial dislocation. And when all is said and done, the reputation of any business enterprise must stand or fall on its long-term influence. Whether the firm's failure was a cause or result of the 1810 slump is of far less consequence than the important part it had played in raising a large part of the funds needed for the struggle against France and in helping to mold the London money market during a vital formative period. Viewed in perspective, the Goldsmid ventures must be regarded as yet another chapter in the frequently neglected story of the Jewish impact on the economic development of modern Britain.

18

THE RISE
OF THE ROTHSCHILDS

The financial influence of the Jews on the outcome of the French Revolution and Napoleon's military adventures is one of those debatable subjects about which it is dangerous to be dogmatic. Yet there is little doubt that during the early phases of that era the firm of Benjamin and Abraham Goldsmid had been very influential in placing the British war effort on a sound financial footing. Even more decisive in this respect during the closing stages were the Rothschilds, who were to become the greatest international merchant bankers of the nineteenth century and play a prominent role in securing Jewish emancipation from civil disabilities.

But because the Rothschilds took great pains to guard their important business affairs, a host of legends and sheer fairy tales have accumulated, making it extremely difficult to arrive at a dispassionate assessment of their significance. In the realm of finance, however, it would seem that they created little that was really new: three centuries earlier wealthy families with far-flung connections and branch houses, like the Fuggers, the Medici, and the Bardi, had flourished, while the internationalization of stock exchange activities—singled out by Sombart as the Rothschilds' special contribution—

probably owed much more to the spread of the joint-stock form of enterprise than it did to any aptitudes displayed by individual speculators.

On the other hand, possibly no group of men exerted more sway over the course of events in Europe between 1810 and 1815—and therein lies the real historical significance of the Rothschild brothers.

To ease their tasks of identification and tax collection, during the eighteenth century the authorities of Frankfurt on the Main had compelled the inhabitants of the *Judengasse* to place distinctive emblems on their houses, and the Rothschild family acquired its name from the red *(rot)* shield *(Schild)* that marked its home. It was in this German ghetto that the firm's founder, Meyer Amschel, was born in 1743.

The free city of Frankfurt, enjoying easy access to the Rhine, had long been a major entrepôt for the principal trade routes of western and central Germany. Its fairs attracted buyers from many regions, and it was a great center for the distribution of foreign—especially British—goods to Württemberg, Saxony, and Bavaria. A good deal of old-fashioned money dealing and banking were carried on here, and Meyer Amschel Rothschild, after gradually acquiring "a collection of pieces" and setting up as a dealer in old coins, went on to become a money changer and to handle some petty brokerage business for the landgrave of Hesse-Cassel. Nevertheless, though its prosperity steadily increased, as late as 1806 the firm was still of little account beyond the immediate business world of Frankfurt itself. In fact, the subsequent soaring fortunes of the family were not the product of Meyer but of his five energetic and resourceful sons, who had grown up in the cramped quarters of the *Judengasse*.

One of them, Nathan Meyer, had settled in the bustling metropolis of Manchester, England, in 1797, where he engaged in the purchase of semiprocessed cottons, arranged for the dyeing and cutting, and dispatched the finished cloth to the parent firm at home, together with colonial produce, such as indigo, sugar, and coffee. Deciding to settle in England for good, he moved his business to London in 1804 and became a naturalized British subject two years later.

Up to that time father and sons had created a modest merchandising business, coupled with bill-of-exchange and petty banking operations; but they were not much more than a third-rate firm. Soon, however, and particularly after 1810, a shrewd ability for exploiting to maximum advantage certain circumstances engendered by the war situation was to carry the Rothschilds to unimagined heights of affluence.

The defeat at Trafalgar had put an end to Napoleon's plans for a direct invasion of Britain and, to a considerable extent, had transformed the Anglo-French struggle from a military to an economic contest. In the autumn of 1806, after Prussia had fallen, the Berlin Decree proclaimed the British Isles to be in a state of blockade, and the signatures of Austria, Russia, Sweden, and Denmark were soon added to this scheme of commercial warfare. There now ensued a long and intense struggle between the emperor's resolve to exclude British and colonial produce from the Continent—hence the name continental system—and the determination of the peoples of Europe themselves (backed by British counterblockade measures) to secure such supplies, even at greatly inflated prices.

This was a situation offering enormous scope to the entrepreneurial initiative of any businessman lucky enough to have a footing in both camps. Among the few in this fortunate position were the Rothschilds (for Frankfurt was now part of the French-dominated Confederation of the Rhine), and under Nathan's skillful guidance the firm plunged into the cross-channel contraband trade with all its energies.

Even greater opportunities for profit presented themselves when Napoleon's blockade (under which neutrals and French allies were not to trade with the British) began to have a boomerang effect and he found it necessary to regularize the illicit traffic after 1810 to insure a supply of essential commodities. In effect, the French authorities now began to compete with the illegal traders, admitting contraband articles under license on the payment of duties calculated to be just below the cost of smuggling.

Nathan took advantage of this officially sanctioned clandestine commerce to do business on an extensive scale, both on his own account and on behalf of the Frankfurt firm. The kingpin in these arrangements was James, his youngest brother, who had set up a Rothschild agency in Paris itself in 1811, where he had soon won the esteem and confidence of the authorities. James oscillated continually between the French capital and the port of Gravelines, where licensed articles from England could be off-loaded under police supervision. It is more than probable that these activities served mainly as a cloak for large-scale smuggling operations and an enormously profitable traffic in commercial bills.

Thus the undermining of Napoleon's continental system proved to be one of the three pillars on which the fortunes of the house of Rothschild were originally built.

Meanwhile, the center of military interest had come to be focused on Britain's diversionary campaign led by the duke of Wellington on the Iberian Peninsula. If this plan was to succeed, however, the duke had to receive adequate funds for paying his troops and for purchasing local supplies, since he could not afford to alienate the sympathies of the Spaniards by living on the country. Yet there could be no question of shipping the necessary bullion to Lisbon, eight hundred miles from the nearest English port across seas infested with enemy warships and privateers.

For some time Wellington had depended on the services of Maltese and Sicilian money dealers, borrowing silver from them at high rates in exchange for bills on the British Treasury—a procedure that made everything purchased on the peninsula several times more expensive than even the inflated war prices then prevailing. By 1810 the duke was spending at the rate of £200,000 a month, and when Whitehall protested at this heavy outlay, he intimated that it might be wise to abandon the whole project on the grounds of cost. And without the support of Wellington's new-model infantry, Spanish guerrilla resistance wo··ld almost certainly have collapsed, thereby once again exposing Britain herself to the danger of direct invasion. When Nathan Rothschild, with the help of his brothers on the mainland, reversed the financial process, this danger was averted.

Precisely how he managed to do this is by no means altogether clear; apparently he had acquired very cheaply a large slice of Wellington's bills, and after cashing these he shipped the specie to James, who made deposits with various Parisian banks; through a complex network of bill operations (handled in the main by Jewish brokers), notes were then transmitted to Wellington for conversion into silver by local bankers.

While this traffic in Wellington's bills was undoubtedly profitable, the firm's earnings were limited because of the numerous intermediaries through whose hands such transactions had to pass. In fact, the main importance of these dealings was the manner in which they rocketed Nathan to prominence in London financial circles; by 1811 he had come to be recognized there "as the most eminent merchant associated with the trade between this country and the continent" (Edwin Cannan, *The Paper Pound, 1797–1821* [London, 1921], p. 20) and had been called upon to give expert evidence before the House of Commons Bullion Committee.

Top left: Rothschild house in Frankfurt; top right: Meyer Anselm Rothschild; at bottom are Nathan Meyer (left) and Baron James de Rothschild

Having been accepted by the Establishment, Nathan used his astute speculative abilities to the full: gathering together all the liquid funds he could lay his hands on, he purchased at an auction a cargo of gold brought to London by an East India Company vessel; the commissary-general, still desperately short of specie for Wellington, offered to take it over. After quickly disposing of this bullion at a handsome profit, Nathan was then asked to handle the transmission. Subsequently he was to recall: "When the Government had got the money, they did not know how to get it to Portugal. I undertook all that, and I sent it through France. It was the best business I ever did."

Once again, the actual methods used remain somewhat hazy, though James in Paris (now on intimate terms with Napoleon's finance minister, Mollien) must have played a vital part. It is certain, however, that during 1813 alone cash remittances to Spain and Portugal amounted to not less than £1,400,000, the great bulk of which was managed by the Rothschilds.

Handling the money traffic to Wellington, therefore, formed the second pillar supporting the Jewish firm's mushrooming wealth.

The struggle against Napoleon also involved the regular transfer of considerable sums from Britain to her continental allies—mainly in the form of out-and-out subsidies rather than loans. This business was to become the third pillar on which Rothschild financial leadership came to rest.

Following the French retreat from Moscow, Whitehall became anxious to create a grand alliance that would lead to the final overthrow of Napoleon. But if these allies were to place large new levies of troops in the field, the Treasury would have to remit more than £2 million to the Austrians, about half that amount to Russia, and at least £700,000 to the almost-bankrupt Prussians. Because of Britain's seriously depleted reserves bullion itself could not be sent, and a direct remission of bills was likely to have a disastrous impact on the delicate mechanism of the foreign exchanges, leading to a rapid external depreciation of sterling.

In an effort to overcome this problem the Treasury once more called upon the services of Nathan Rothschild. The Jew's talent for financial manipulation in the grand manner now found its fullest expression: in close cooperation with his four brothers on the Continent, Nathan manipulated all the technical devices by which foreign money might be obtained without undue pressure being exerted on sterling, purchasing the largest possible supply of European bills and feeding these into the bill market at regular intervals to maintain an equilibrium. As a consequence, the financial operations essential for the defeat of Napoleon were carried out without any further notable drain of bullion from Britain and with stability in the foreign price of sterling currency.

By the time the "little corporal" had been banished to Elba, the firm enjoyed enormous resources and prestige, although it is extremely difficult to gauge what the Rothschilds were worth, since apparently no accurate estimate of their wealth in 1814 exists. Yet most of the reliable authorities agree that the brothers were now among the richest, if not *the* richest, men in Europe. Solomon, who had served as the principal link between London and Berlin, became commercial adviser to the Prussian government. A destitute count of Provence, soon to travel from exile in Buckinghamshire to be crowned Louis XVIII, took up a loan of 5 million francs with James. From Schönbrunn Palace outside Vienna came a Hapsburg patent conferring a title of nobility on Amschel, the eldest of the brothers, in recognition of his services in transmitting the British subsidies. Karl went to Italy as financial consultant to the king of Naples. Nathan, the astutest of them all, remained in London to launch the firm to new heights of financial eminence with the flotation of postwar government loans and to become immortalized in a verse by Byron as the one who held "the balance of the world."

In the space of five years these five extraordinary brothers had bridged the gulf between the medieval ghetto and the modern world of international finance.

What particular qualities had enabled the Rothschilds to reach this pinnacle in such a brief period? Three attributes —all of them stemming directly from the family's Jewishness —seem to have contributed most to their success.

In the first place, because of their Jewish background and traditions their business outlook was cosmopolitan. The firm transcended war-wasted frontiers to become, in effect, an unofficial but highly resourceful international clearinghouse. Even had the final triumph been Napoleon's, the brothers would have remained prosperous, for they had taken excellent care to protect themselves against any eventuality: while Nathan busied himself in England, Amschel and Solomon were on friendly terms with the French satellite rulers in Germany, and James, as has been noted, was firmly entrenched in Paris itself. "They played the game safe and were in a position to capitalize on victory for either side" (J. T. Flynn, *Men of Wealth* [New York, 1941], pp. 125–26). (Very much later in the nineteenth century, with the immersion of members of the third generation in the mainstream of their various national environments, the house of Rothschild split into a series of separate firms and gradually lost most of its international economic character.)

Second, there was their singleness of purpose. At a time when money was beginning to count more than race or religion in ruling circles, the brothers' overriding ambition was to reach a commercial or financial goal quicker and more effectively than others. Never missing any opportunity for profit, they made themselves indispensable to those with power and connections. In this way they became well placed to collect inside information and to transmit such tidings swiftly to the point at which they could be put to best use—just as Jacob Fugger had done three hundred years before. However, the tale that it was Nathan's courier, outdistancing Wellington's dispatches, who brought the first news of Waterloo to London seems rather farfetched.

The third factor in the Rothschild success story might be summed up as Jewish family feeling—an intangible that went very much beyond mere clannishness. Referring in general terms to the triumphs of certain firms at this time, Jenks has argued that "it was those businessmen who like the Quakers and the Jews most tempered their individualism with an older economic tradition, the community of the family, who most persistently throve" (op. cit., pp. 20–21). In the Rothschilds' case, the five sons shared equally in the profit and loss of every transaction while the father was alive; and when Meyer Amschel died in 1812 his will provided that only these brothers were to have an interest in the business (he was survived by five daughters also). In this way, the enterprise would be less likely to become imperiled by the possible follies of one member, inactive relatives would be unable to sponge and make withdrawals of essential assets, and—again, like Jacob Fugger—a continuing dynasty of active male heirs would be created, in recognition of the concept that the firm should be an entity distinct and separate from the individuals who directed its affairs.

In many ways the most striking phenomenon of the age after Napoleon himself was the Rothschild brothers; and in no small measure their greatness flowed from characteristics that were essentially Jewish.

19

THE DON PACIFICO
AFFAIR

History provides few instances of individual Jewish businessmen exercising a decisive influence on diplomatic and political events. However, there was one mid-nineteenth century
occasion, now almost forgotten, when the private affairs of a
Jewish merchant not only caused the near-downfall of a British cabinet and established the reputation of Lord Palmerston as one of the greatest parliamentary debaters of his time,
but also generated a first-class international rumpus that
brought the major European powers to the brink of war. Yet
the surprising thing about the person who started the whole
affair is that he was hardly of the Goldsmid or Rothschild
caliber—in fact, he was something of a charlatan and petty
scalawag.

David (popularly known as Don) Pacifico was a Portuguese
Jew who, because of the accident that he had been born at
Gibraltar in 1784, was able to claim he was a British subject.
From 1812 he carried on a merchandising business in the
seaport of Lagos, in south Portugal, later moving to Mertola,
an inland market town on the Guadiana River. His property
in Mertola was confiscated by Dom Miguel during the civil
war of 1828–33 because he had supported the liberal faction,

and Pacifico moved to the Barbary Coast. Following the overthrow of the Miguel regime he was appointed Portuguese consul in Morocco in 1835. Between 1837 and 1842 he served as Portuguese consul-general in Greece, thereafter remaining in Athens as a merchant.

Greece had only recently gained political independence from the Ottoman Empire, its sovereignty being jointly guaranteed by Britain, France, and Russia. The predominantly Jewish city and port of Salonika, however, stayed under Turkish rule, becoming a keen competitor to the burgeoning Greek maritime trade centered on Piraeus, the harbor of Athens. The centuries-old religious anti-Semitism of Hellas was now inflamed by commercial rivalry, and anti-Jewish outbursts in the Greek capital were not infrequent, in spite of the fact that Jews were recognized by the new state as full citizens.

During Easter of 1847 the Greek authorities banned the customary burning of Judas Iscariot in effigy, out of deference to Baron Rothschild, who was then visiting Athens. Deprived of this traditional auto-da-fé, the Athenian mob (instigated, it was alleged subsequently, by the sons of the minister of war) turned on David Pacifico's house—which happened to stand near the spot where the burning usually took place—and set fire to the dwelling and its contents.

The Jewish merchant naturally demanded and was fully entitled to compensation. Pacifico, however, who by all reports had always lived in a modest fashion and was known to be in financial difficulties, assessed his claims on a fanciful scale: he argued that the mob had looted rare curios that had been painstakingly collected over many years, that valuable brocade furniture had been gutted, and that his wife and daughters had lost jewelry worth £2000. But this bill for household and personal property was dwarfed by the value set on certain vouchers destroyed in the riot, which he alleged to have been evidences of outstanding debts owed him by the Portuguese government amounting to £26,000. When the Greek authorities refused to countenance these claims, Pacifico, by a happy thought, remembered the site of his birth and resolved to appeal for redress to the Foreign Office at Whitehall on the grounds that he was a British subject.

For several years prior to this incident disappointment had been mounting in London at the behavior of the Athenian administration. The property of other British subjects residing in Greece (including the historian George Finlay) had been sequestered, members of British crews had been maltreated in Greek ports, repayments of British loans had been arbitrarily suspended—and there were no signs of a settlement over compensation for these and other grievances. Moreover, Lord Palmerston, the foreign minister, firmly believed that both France and Russia were tacitly supporting Greek recalcitrance in these matters.

The Pacifico affair, therefore, provided Palmerston with a welcome pretext to adopt a more forceful policy in Greek affairs. After nearly three years of futile palaver, in the course of which the foreign minister fully endorsed every one of the Jewish merchant's exaggerated demands, Palmerston took the decisive step of instructing the Admiralty to dispatch the Mediterranean fleet from the Dardanelles to Athens. Fifteen British battleships, under Admiral Sir William Parker, anchored in Salamis Bay in mid-January 1850, and Ambassador Wyse presented an ultimatum to King Otto; when this was rejected, a blockade of Piraeus was ordered so that sufficient Greek shipping could be seized to cover payment of Pacifico's claims.

The intimidated and browbeaten Greeks thereupon offered to negotiate, but Palmerston was not prepared to discuss either the justice of the Jew's demands or to haggle over the amount: "If these cases [he declared bluntly] have multiplied during the last two or three years beyond all former example, it is in consequence of the prevalence of the notion that British subjects may be wronged with impunity, and that the British Government will not stir hand or foot to help them. It is not so with French or North American citizens, and no state ventures to ill-use a Russian. . . . We must have money . . . and not promises to pay. These promises would infallibly be broken, and we should have to begin all over again" (quoted in W. B. Pemberton, *Lord Palmerston* [London, 1954], pp. 167–68).

The Athenian authorities finally yielded to Palmerston's steamroller tactics on April 26: Don Pacifico was to receive an immediate payment of 120,000 drachmas (about £4,200) for his losses and as compensation for the personal injuries and sufferings to himself and his family; moreover, a further sum of 150,000 drachmas was to be handed over by King Otto's government as a security deposit while a mixed commission of British, French, and Greek officials in Lisbon investigated the question of the damage incurred through the destruction of the documents establishing Pacifico's alleged claim against the Portuguese.

"The spoilt child of absolutism" (as Palmerston called Otto) had now received deserved chastisement for years of defiance and insults.

The affair was by no means at an end, however; in fact, the fun was just beginning. It was hardly to be expected that France and Russia—the other guarantors of Greek independence—would take kindly to the assumption that the British had the right to blockade Greek ports unilaterally. When Palmerston rejected a French offer of mediation, the French ambassador was withdrawn from London, and anti-British feelings across the Channel became so strong that there was much talk of war.

This rupture with France coincided with the dispatch of a

strongly worded memorandum by Count Nesselrode (the Russian chancellor) to the Foreign Office, protesting the coercion of small states by British maritime power and inquiring "whether Great Britian, abusing the advantages afforded by her immense maritime superiority, intends henceforth to pursue an isolated policy . . . and to authorize all Great Powers on every fitting opportunity to recognize toward the weak no other rule but their own will." Although Palmerston sent a very mild and conciliatory reply, the Russian ambassador refused to attend a dinner party that the foreign secretary had arranged in honor of the queen's birthday.

As diplomatic relations with the continental powers became more envenomed over the Pacifico incident, Palmerston began to lose the support of his own cabinet colleagues, and English diarist Charles Greville's *Memoirs* teem with evidence of this fact; writing on May 19, 1850, for instance, Greville jubilantly says: "There is the devil to pay about this Greek affair, and at last there seems a tolerable chance of Palmerston coming to grief."

The government's Tory opponents were quick to take advantage of this situation, and on June 17 Lord Stanley moved a vote of censure in the House of Lords. With deep sarcasm he cut Palmerston's Greek policy to pieces, somewhat unfairly denouncing Pacifico himself as "this petty usurer trading on a borrowed capital of thirty pounds" and describing the foreign minister's actions as "calculated to endanger the continuance of our friendly relations with other Powers." Stanley's resolution carried by 169 to 132; the ministry was on the verge of toppling, as London's most influential newspaper thundered that British foreign policy under Palmerston had "degenerated into a tissue of caprices, machinations, petty contentions and everlasting disputes."

As things turned out, however, by raising the Pacifico issue in the upper house the Opposition had blundered tactically.

Stanley's victory led to a closing of cabinet ranks, and Russell's government, instead of resigning or dropping Palmerston, resolved to throw itself on the mercy of a general debate in the House of Commons. The Don Pacifico inquest that followed (June 24–28) was one of the most sensational debates in the whole history of Parliament: not only did it include the greatest of all Palmerston's speeches, but also the first major Commons peroration by Gladstone and Sir Robert Peel's last speech (he was thrown from his horse a few days later and died of the injuries). Disraeli, Russell, and Cobden all took an active part.

The climax came on the second evening when the foreign minister rose to address a crowded and excited house; his speech lasted for nearly five hours, though all he held in his hand was a half sheet of writing paper. From this sustained effort only a few salient extracts can be given. The House of Lords' resolution, he argued, implied "that British subjects abroad must not look to their own country for protection, but must trust to that indifferent justice which they may happen to receive at the hands of the government and tribunals of the country in which they may be."

Palmerston rejected the validity of this proposition and proceeded to turn to good account the ridicule that had been heaped on David Pacifico—his dubious early career, his costly furniture, and his paper claims. Indignantly he denied the suggestion that because a man cut a ridiculous figure he was a person with whom a foreign government need not deal fairly: "I know nothing of the truth or falsehood of these stories . . . but I don't care what his character is . . . I do not, and cannot admit, that because a man may have done amiss on some other occasion, and in some other matter, he is to be wronged with impunity by others. The rights of a man depend on the merits of the particular case."

And he went on to protest against the house being kept "in

a roar of laughter at the poverty of one sufferer, or at the miserable habitation of another; at the nationality of one man, or the religion of another; as if because a man is poor he might be bastinadoed and tortured with impunity . . . or because a man is of the Jewish persuasion he is a fair mark for any outrage."

Ultimately, however, Palmerston's appeal—addressed to the patriotic pride of his fellow countrymen—proved irresistible: "I therefore fearlessly challenge the verdict which this House, as representing a political, a commercial, a constitutional country, is to give on the question now brought before it—whether the principles on which the foreign policy of Her Majesty's Government has been conducted, and the sense of duty which has led us to think ourselves bound to afford protection to our fellow-subjects abroad, are proper and fitting guides for those who are charged with the Government of England; and whether, as the Roman in days of old held himself free from indignity when he could say, *civis Romanus sum,* so also a British subject, in whatever land he may be, shall feel confident that the watchful eye and the strong arm of England will protect him against injustice and wrong."

Much of the remainder of the debate was an anticlimax. Gladstone argued that the question of Pacifico's character was fundamental, since the claims rested "altogether on his personal credit"—yet the Jew had made no effort to secure civil redress. And his "celebrated inventory" was patently false, because a person who was known to have had to borrow a mere £30 from the Bank of Athens was hardly likely to possess luxurious furniture, clothes, and jewels. As for the major claim of £26,000, which had been pending for twenty-nine years against the Portuguese government, why, Gladstone asked, had Pacifico never once invoked the aid of the British minister in Lisbon, but only raised the matter as an afterthought when the alleged bonds had been destroyed?

Disraeli, whose main concern was the restoration of amiable relations with France, also brushed aside Pacifico's claims as "doubtful in their character and exaggerated in their amount," and went on to surprise the House of Commons with a contemptuous reference to the Jews of Gibraltar as "a teeming and scheming race, not distinguished by the highest morality."

Despite all the eloquence and logic of these skillful opponents, the popular note which Palmerston had struck won out, and a vote of confidence in the government's foreign policy was carried by 310 to 264. It was not a triumph of oratory in the conventional sense: as a speaker Palmerston was full of "hums" and "haws," and his voice trailed away before the end of a sentence, the pause being filled by a flourish of his handkerchief. Rather, it was a triumph of character. With his dyed whiskers and red face, Palmerston had become the living embodiment of John Bull, the man who would stand no nonsense from any foreign government. The jubilant Whigs gave the foreign secretary a dinner at the Reform Club and presented him with his portrait for "the independent policy by which he has maintained the honour and interests of this country," while even his bitterest adversaries admitted that his speech had been a masterpiece.

Long after the echoes of these statesmen in Westminster had died away, ripples from the Don Pacifico affair continued to lap against the troubled shores of European diplomacy. Although Palmerston soon found the means of mollifying France, there can be little doubt that relations with Russia (already strained by other conflicts) were further exacerbated by this episode and festered slowly, erupting in the Crimean War. Moreover, in many quarters of the Continent, Palmerston's actions and his *civis Romanus sum* speech seemed perfect expressions of arrogant and confident British imperial pride. In Greece itself the despotic Otto for the first time gained some measure of popular support through the stand he had taken, and nationalism was rekindled (the officers of the Athenian garrison went so far as to surrender half their pay as a contribution toward the compensation money). It is certain, too, that anti-Semitic elements in the Balkans (especially in Romania and Bulgaria) were emboldened by the whole business. On the other hand, in England the public and parliamentary controversy, and particularly Palmerston's stout defense of Pacifico's inherent rights, helped to create a favorable climate for the sweeping away of remaining Jewish civil disabilities.

The incident also marked the beginning of a long struggle between those who (like Palmerston himself) rationalized their expansionist ambitions by arguing that Britain, the natural guardian of liberty, was obliged to assert her ideas and make her influence felt, and those (like Gladstone) who believed that such policies would set all Europe by the ears and who favored instead the principle of nonintervention. Having become the workshop of the world, the United Kingdom had to remain on good terms with all foreigners, whom it needed as customers, and this could hardly be achieved by unceasing interference in their domestic affairs. In fact, the Don Pacifico episode can be regarded as an early manifestation of the economic imperialism that all the major European powers practiced so widely later in that century (one important aspect of which was to protect and further the interests of nationals living abroad by force).

And what of the two principal figures in the affair: Palmerston and Pacifico? Ever since her foreign secretary had almost ruined her pet project of holding the Great Exhibition in Hyde Park, Queen Victoria had not been very favorably disposed toward "Old Pam," and the June debate provided her with a pretext to send him a memorandum that amounted to a demand for him to cease acting on his own initiative in foreign affairs. Palmerston replied evasively and carried on as before, until (much to the queen's delight) he was dismissed from the Foreign Office in 1852 for indiscreetly expressing personal approval of Louis Napoleon's coup d'etat. But the sixty-eight-year-old statesman was soon back in harness again, first at the Home Office and then as prime minister. Soon after the beginning of his second tenure in Downing Street the Jewish Disabilities Bill was passed (July 1858).

Meanwhile, the joint British-French-Greek commission, working in Lisbon, had found the originals of the Jewish merchant's lost documents in the Portuguese archives, on the basis of which it assessed the amount still outstanding, together with the expenses incurred by him during the investigation; it came to only £150. That sum was paid by the Hellenic government to the British minister at Athens on June 13, 1851. Thus ended a career which for a brief moment had become enmeshed in the web of great events, for after David Pacifico received this final installment of his claims he disappeared from the limelight of history. All that is known of his later life is that he finally settled in Bury Street, London, where he died in April 1854 and was buried in the Spanish Jews' cemetery, which still skirts the Regent's Canal off Mile End Road.

20

MARCUS SAMUEL
OIL GIANT
OF BRITISH JEWRY

The history of modern international "tycoonery" has often been very closely associated with the great pioneers in petroleum—an industry which has so enormously influenced present-day living that without oil and its numerous by-products the economies of most countries would simply grind to a standstill. And certainly few would deny that one of the most significant case studies in the development of American big business over the past century is provided by the story of John D. Rockefeller and the Standard Oil Company. Though it had repercussions of a similar magnitude, the growth and spread of the Shell emblem during the bustling early phase of petroleum production is a much less familiar tale.

At first the sign of the shell had nothing whatever to do with the new source of energy. Victorian society had an inordinate fondness for bric-a-brac of all kinds, and when the monopolistic charter of the East India Company was abrogated in 1834, thereby opening up the China seas to private vessels, an astute London Jew, Marcus Samuel, began purchasing coral, mother-of-pearl, and other exotic seashells from returning sailors and ships' captains. He would clean and polish these wares in a little workshop in Upper East Smithfield and convert them into shell boxes, trinkets, and other souvenirs for sale to the wholesalers who supplied the esplanade booths of the seaside towns and the curio stalls of the inland spas. Such was the prevailing appetite for seashell products that within twenty years Samuel and his family had progressed from near poverty to relative wealth.

When Marcus Samuel the younger was born in 1853 his father already was quite a prosperous trader who now placed regular purchase orders with the big merchant houses of the City, which had agencies in the Far East. But when his father died in 1870 the family business was left to Joseph, the oldest of three sons, who was an unenterprising, conservative businessman.

Marcus (who had enjoyed a good education at a Jewish school in Brussels) and his other brother, Sam, went into partnership on their own account, though their resources were negligible. But the currents of history were flowing favorably, and the development of the oriental trade, the conversion from sail to steam, the opening of the Suez Canal, and the birth of industrial Japan were all to play a part in the rise of M. Samuel & Co.

Young Marcus Samuel set out on his first voyage to the Far East in 1873. Although only a youth of nineteen, with little cash or credit, he succeeded in chartering fifty thousand tons of shipping for bringing surplus rice from Siam to famine-stricken Bengal. Behind this first operation lay the very simple commercial principle on which all subsequent plans were to be based: the principle of seeking the nearest source of supply to match a local demand.

His second trip eastward, begun in 1876, took him around the world via Hong Kong, Japan, San Francisco, and Montreal. But unlike Jules Verne's hero Phileas Fogg, who traced a similar course, Marcus sought knowledge, experience, and valuable contacts rather than mere adventure. Using the fruits of these travels as a base for operations, Marcus and Sam began conducting regular business with the Orient.

After less than a decade the partnership was held in such high esteem that long-established houses in the Far Eastern trade (such as Jardine Matheson) were recommending the Samuels to the Paris branch of the Rothschilds. Meanwhile, in return for exports of machinery the firm was busy introducing cheap Japanese lacquer, carvings, and chinaware into thousands of middle-class homes where taste was dictated by fashion rather than by artistic judgment. The brothers, in fact, had come to play a leading role in the growth of Anglo-Japanese trade relations.

Although the Samuels' business with Japan covered a very wide field, it was their traffic in coal from Yokohama to Malaya and Indonesia that first drew their attention to the extensive demand for oil in those parts. All the early oil wars were fought over the world markets for kerosene or lamp oil; it was only after the turn of the century that the growth in the number of automobiles justified campaigns over petroleum. However, while he learned about the tremendous scope for the "new light," Marcus Samuel learned also that the refining, transport, and marketing of mineral oil in the Far East was firmly in the hands of Rockefeller's Standard Oil monopoly—a bastion too powerful to be breached unless an interloper could find some means of reducing costs so drastically that Standard would be undersold without being able to afford to retaliate.

With this premise in mind, Marcus devised an ingenious scheme to gain a footing in international oil. First, with the aid of the Rothschilds he procured supplies of Russian kerosene. Then in order to avoid the long and expensive haul around the Cape of Good Hope, Samuel set Newcastle ship-builders the task of designing tankers that would meet the strict safety requirements of the Suez Canal governors; at the same time these vessels were to be fitted with steam-cleaning equipment that would enable them to take on freights of general cargo after discharging their oil, so that they need not return empty. And third, a comprehensive storage and distribution system was created through setting up bulk stations at strategic points in the Far East and operating these in conjunction with refineries.

The first bulk shipment of the new oil passed through Suez in the summer of 1892 on the *Murex;* by the end of the following year a fleet of eleven tankers (all of them named after shells) was in operation, costs had been cut so effectively that not even Standard could afford to undersell, and Marcus Samuel had not only become a very rich man but also a major figure in the world of oil.

Obviously such an elaborate and revolutionary project in oil marketing was far beyond the resources of the Samuel firm itself. Between 1892 and 1897 Marcus was at the head of a group known as the Tank Syndicate, which comprised all the merchants in the Far East through whom the bulk oil flowing from Baku was distributed. This syndicate arrangement enabled Marcus and Sam to run their rapidly expanding business without specialized departments, without expensive foreign agents, and with a staff that otherwise would have been wholly inadequate.

Yet no enterprise, however admirably it worked at very little cost, could afford to ignore the benefits of joint-stock organization, and in February 1898 the Tank Syndicate became the nucleus of the Shell Transport and Trading Company Limited, with a capital of £1,800,000; Marcus was chairman. This consolidation had been motivated in part by

Samuel's determination to secure freedom from dependence on Russian oil, the price of which had begun to fluctuate wildly and unpredictably. Since all sources in the New World were still controlled by Standard, Marcus's search was directed to the only other major supplies known at the time: the East Indies.

An allied Dutch firm had already made an inauspicious beginning in southeastern Borneo, but the first oil struck there was so heavy and so low in kerosene content that a Standard Oil observer commented: "A great bluff or an awful mistake is being perpetrated." But Marcus Samuel was not a bluffer: new strikes of lighter oil were made, and within a few months the first shipment of Indonesian kerosene was on its way northward through Suez. Soon a modern refinery was constructed in eastern Borneo, capable of handling a million tons of crude oil annually.

Intelligent risk-spreading rather than a single-minded devotion to oil accounted for much of Shell's initial success. As Marcus himself pointed out at the first annual meeting of shareholders: "This company are largely dependent upon their trade as carriers rather than as oil merchants for their earning powers."

In spite of the company's heavy investments in its Borneo properties, profits by mid-1900 had increased by 60 percent and £100 shares of Shell were worth £300. Inevitably high earnings attract competitors, and very soon the Royal Dutch firm, under the wily Henri Deterding, was impinging upon Samuel's oil empire in the Far East. A lengthy, complex price war ensued, until in 1903 Deterding persuaded Marcus to enter into an agreement with Royal Dutch and the Paris house of Rothschild (the latter representing Russian oil interests). This cartel led in turn to the establishment of the Asiatic Petroleum Company to carry out joint marketing arrangements—the upshot of which was to drive Standard almost completely from the European scene.

Four years later Royal Dutch and Shell came even closer together, and a period of intricate arrangements and rearrangements, share exchanges, and holding companies set in. Out of this welter of intercompany financing Marcus emerged, as he himself put it, "a disappointed man," for when the merger was complete, Deterding held the whip hand as managing director; the forty-sixty relationship established then remains the basic structure of the Royal Dutch–Shell group today.

Always a good loser, Marcus bore Deterding no ill will and, in fact, conceded victory to the Dutchman with these words: "I am going to pay you the highest possible compliment. You ought to have been a Jew." To the world at large, however, it now seemed as if Samuel's meteoric business career was finished. In fact, with the Dutch in ultimate control, he thought so himself, for although he remained chairman of Shell, he commented: "I do not see the use of continuing work for the mere purpose of moneymaking, having realized long ago quite as much as I need." As things turned out Marcus had been too pessimistic; the merger did not result in complete domination by the Dutch, and it was Samuel— as leader of the British element in the group—who continued to be regarded (both by governments and other oil competitors) as head of the whole Anglo-Dutch combine and to be dubbed by the press the "Napoleon of oil" and the "European Rockefeller."

Though the structure of the new combine represented a sore defeat for Marcus, he was to rise from the Dutch-British amalgamation to far greater triumphs than ever before. In newspaper interviews he was always fond of stressing what he regarded as the secret of success: if one wanted to reach the top, he pointed out, it was essential to have new ideas that were not mere gimmicks but had a fundamental impact. His own fresh schemes were to prove of great national importance.

Ever since boyhood Marcus had cherished a passionate affection for the British navy. His knowledge of the oil business had led him to start a fifteen-year campaign for the conversion of warships from coal to liquid fuel. At first his pleas fell on deaf ears. Meanwhile, the Admiralty, fearing German naval parity, had placed orders for the construction of twenty super-dreadnoughts. These giant warships, costing £3 million apiece, began service about the same time that the submarine and torpedo boat appeared on the scene, and because they were slow and expensive to maintain, the dreadnoughts were threatened with obsolescence from the start.

Samuel's solution offered the only way out: if speed was not to be sacrificed to size, the new warships had to be driven by marine fuel, which provided 40 percent more energy than did a similar weight of coal. Moreover, oil made it far easier to reach full speed, and refueling on the open sea not only was a much quicker process but also required fewer hands. These arguments in favor of an oil-burning navy were unanswerable, and Samuel, with the support of the unpopular Lord Fisher, finally won his battle despite intense Admiralty opposition.

His other great contribution toward ultimate victory over the Central Powers concerned toluol, a chemical essential for the manufacture of TNT explosives. By 1916 the U.S. War Department had become gravely perturbed by the extreme shortage of this substance in both Britain and France, whereas the distillation of their brown coal gave the Germans a practically unlimited source. Marcus, however, was able to convince the authorities that Borneo crude oil was exceptionally rich in toluol, and he threw himself into the extremely difficult task of organizing adequate supplies. It was an action deserving a niche in history at least as great as Chaim Weizmann's for the production of acetone at the same critical stage of the war.

Born in London's teeming East End and reared in a society which, while allowing Jews to live in peace and prosperity, didn't quite accept them, Marcus Samuel became a tycoon of the Rockefeller caliber but with a different set of values. Not once did he follow the traditional custom in international oil politics: that of moving in and ruthlessly destroying his opponents when he held all the right cards in his hand. In 1919, when he gave up personal control of the board, the value of his holdings in Shell amounted to more than £7 million, but this enormous wealth had not been acquired as an end in itself. Through community service Samuel was determined to achieve every recognition available to a British citizen; and in order to gain such complete acceptance he had to become rich and commercially powerful.

In 1903, having served as alderman and sheriff, he became London's third Jewish lord mayor. Accompanied by music provided by the Jews' Orphan Asylum, he insisted on diverting the procession for his installation to Whitechapel. There, in the heart of the East End, Samuel was acclaimed by packed masses of recent immigrants, many with their strange ringlets and foreign ghetto dress and Yiddish talk (which Marcus did not understand)—and all living in the semisqualor to which he himself had been born.

As lord mayor he received his first hereditary title: a baronetcy; from World War I he emerged as a respected elder statesman; and in the birthday honors of 1925 he was elevated to the peerage as Viscount Bearsted. But this was not acceptance at any price: when he became lord mayor, for example, he refused to entertain officially the representative of the anti-Jewish Romanian government. Earlier, as an alderman, he had expended tremendous energies in scotching the activities of anti-Semitic elements in London. Naturally, this devotion to public service and the Jewish cause was not always good for business, and his placing of civic duties above the affairs of oil was partly responsible for the successful Royal Dutch coup.

A king on the ruthless battlefield of the early days of oil, Marcus Samuel also bore the stamp of a prince of Israel, and when he died in January 1927 even the thick London fog failed to deter thousands from the poorest quarters of the East End from following the funeral cortege to the Jewish cemetery at Willesden.

VI

NEW
WORLDS

21

JEWISH
ECONOMIC ACTIVITIES
IN COLONIAL BRAZIL

Most people tend to overlook the fact that the Western Hemisphere contains *two* United States. The United States of Brazil covers almost half the continent of South America (that is, an area larger than that of the U.S.A.) and is the fourth largest political unit in the modern world. Yet Brazil today lags far behind Argentina as a center for Jewish settlement in Latin America, having a Jewish community of only 100,000 (out of a total population of more than 80 million).

Nonetheless, the history of Brazilian Jewry goes back to the very beginnings of European penetration in the New World. It is the oldest Jewish community in the Americas, and there was a time when it exerted a considerable influence over the country's development. We would like to examine here the nature of the impact of Jewish colonization on the economic progress of early Brazil.

Having accidentally been discovered by Cabral, who had taken possession of it in the name of the Portuguese crown (April 1500), Brazil was regarded as nothing more than a convenient landfall for the eastward-bound spice fleets prior to their sailing into the belt of the northwesterlies that would blow them around the Cape of Good Hope and into the

Indian Ocean. A few hardy explorers, in search of a westward passage to the Orient, tried to get around or through Brazil, until they discovered that the supposed island was part of a considerable land mass. Preoccupation with the riches of India precluded any major interest in such a vast and virgin territory, and the Portuguese were content with establishing a number of tiny provision stations at the best harbors, sending out small batches of reluctant convict settlers for the purpose. Very soon, however, voluntary pioneers of a more spirited caliber began to arrive.

Toward the close of the fifteenth century the Jews of Portugal still felt reasonably secure: they were rendering valuable services to the crown with their superior talents as tax gatherers, and the authorities could always rely on them for prompt cash loans; among their ranks were skilled craftsmen, some of whom had been responsible for founding the local printing industry; numerous branches of foreign trade were firmly in their hands; and, apart from outbreaks of popular feeling against usury, late medieval Portugal was reasonably free of anti-Semitic violence. In fact, when Ferdinand and Isabella of Spain enforced their edict of expulsion, about sixty thousand Jews (one-third of the total number of refugees) had been given asylum by King John II of Portugal.

Nor did this state of affairs alter very markedly after the accession of Manuel I in 1495; the new king commenced his reign by continuing the policy of leniency toward the Jews. Such clemency, however, was nipped in the bud when it came into conflict with the monarch's matrimonial ambitions. Manuel was bent on marriage with the infanta Isabella of Castile-Aragon, and to that end he was obliged to bring his policy into line with the intolerance practiced across the border. The princess had already turned down a state visit to Lisbon until the king "shall have quite cast the Jews out of his realms." This was not a step that Manuel took lightly, and he shrewdly aimed at striking the best possible bargain for himself. To insure the marriage alliance with Spain he issued an order (December 1496) expelling all Jews who were unwilling to be baptized, under pain of confiscation and death; on the other hand, to forestall losing the fruits of Jewish enterprise altogether, he granted them asylum in distant Brazil, where their presence was unlikely to offend the susceptibilities of his prospective in-laws.

Soon afterward a Portuguese Marrano, Fernando de Noronha, secured a charter to introduce Jewish colonists and to develop the resources of Brazil. By 1503 these settlers (numbering a few dozen at the most) were experiencing severe hardships: the scattered and primitive Indian tribes offered few inducements to potential traders, and, with the exception of dyewoods, only parrots, monkeys, and similar items of curiosity could be exported on the one or two vessels that annually made direct contact with Europe. Like their convict predecessors, some of these Jewish pioneers began to conform to an environment that was beyond their control, took to the ways of the natives, and frequently intermarried with them.

The Cinderella colony received a much-needed boost in 1532 when a small batch of Marrano "penitent heretics" arrived from Madeira. From that island they brought with them some sugarcane plants and, with characteristic energy and initiative, speedily introduced the cultivation of cane along the coastal fringes. By the 1570s sugar had far outstripped dyewoods as the settlement's chief export, and an annual average load of twenty-four hundred hogsheads was crossing the Atlantic. Living on large plantations and making extensive use of local Indian labor and imported Negro slaves, the Jewish sugar planters prospered; as one contemporary traveler put it, "the profits which these New Christians make after being in those lands nine or ten years are marvelous, and some of them are worth 60, 80, or even 100 thousand crowns."

When Spain and Portugal were united in 1580 the tentacles of the Inquisition began to reach out to the Portuguese overseas empire and resulted in the levying of forced loans on the Marrano business communities that had sprung up at Bahia and Pernambuco to serve the sugar industry. Nevertheless, the colonists continued to thrive, and by the turn of the century the plantations, the bulk of the Negro slave trade, more than one hundred sugar mills, and most of the exports of processed sugar were in the hands of Jewish settlers.

The Jewish contribution to Brazil's early economic progress is coming to be increasingly recognized by the Brazilians themselves. For instance, their leading historian, Prof. Gilberto Freyre, has written: "As for the Jew, there is evidence to the effect that he was one of the most active agents in the winning of a market for the sugar-producers of Brazil, a function that, during the first century of colonization, he fulfilled to the great advantage of this part of the Americas. He would appear to have been the most efficient of those technicians responsible for setting up the first sugar mills. The history of patriarchal society in Brazil is, for this reason, inseparable from the history of the Jew in America" (*The Masters and the Slaves* [New York, 1946]).

From the outset the mother country had derived little direct benefit from the sugar export trade, the bulk of which was destined for foreign markets—Holland being by far the most important. In spite of Portuguese prohibitions, by 1620 some fifty thousand chests of Brazilian sugar were annually reaching Amsterdam via Oporto and Lisbon, through the judicious bribery of local officials and the assistance of Marrano agents. It was this clandestine trade that provided the initial impetus for the rise of a great sugar-refining industry in the Dutch capital (in which Amsterdam Jews were especially important), the refined product being reexported to

England, France, and the Baltic lands. In exchange, Brazil had become a valuable export market for Dutch linen fabrics and woolen textiles.

This profitable commerce between the Jewish colonists and Holland was a major factor in the establishment of the Dutch West India Company in 1621 for the purpose of securing a foothold in Brazil. If that could be achieved it would not only result in a great increase in the transatlantic sugar trade, but also the Spanish silver mines in neighboring Peru could be attacked from such a base. Should these treasure deposits fall into Dutch hands, it was argued, the Spaniards would no longer be in a position to finance mercenary armies to oppose the Dutch struggle for complete independence.

There can be little doubt that, in assessing the pros and cons of such an enterprise, the States-General took into account the support that a Dutch landing force was likely to receive from the Jewish and Marrano settlers. Although the evidence is fragmentary, it appears that when the company did launch its Brazilian campaign, both Bahia and Pernambuco were captured with local Jewish assistance; when Bahia was temporarily retaken by the Portuguese in 1625, at least five Jews were executed because of their alleged sympathies toward the invaders. In short, the Jewish pioneers of Brazil now found themselves enmeshed in a web of antagonistic mercantilist colonial ambitions.

By 1640 the West India Company controlled the six northern provinces, including the whole of the sugar-producing area, and hence the main region of Jewish settlement. Nevertheless, direct Jewish participation in the early activities of the company should not be exaggerated. The archival researches of modern historians, such as Hermann Wätjen and I. G. van Dillen, have greatly undermined Sombart's legend that those Marrano exiles from Spain and Portugal who flocked to Amsterdam in the early decades of the seventeenth century provided the bulk of the company's financial resources. In fact, out of a total of some 3 million florins subscribed to the initial capital, the eighteen Jews who invested contributed a mere thirty-six thousand—although complete lists of early company shareholders are lacking.

On the other hand, once the company had begun to achieve its objective (from about 1630 on), Jewish interest and participation in the economic development of Dutch Brazil became considerable.

The Dutch occupation of northern Brazil had two immediate effects on Jewish colonization: first, most of the "New Christians" or Marranos renounced their Catholic adherence and openly proclaimed their traditional faith; second, the community received a great influx of immigrants, not only from Holland, but from such diverse areas as Turkey, the Barbary States, Poland, and Hungary. By 1644 the number of Jews in Dutch Brazil was about fifteen hundred, out of a total white civilian population of just under three thousand.

In order to accelerate the exploitation of the colony's natural resources, thereby providing a further stimulus to Dutch shipping and trading activities across the Atlantic, the authorities permitted a greater degree of religious freedom in Netherlands Brazil than was to be found anywhere else in the Western world at that time. During the governorship of Johann Maurits (1637–44) two synagogues were built in Pernambuco, and the friars were soon protesting that the Jews were busy converting local Christians to the Mosaic faith.

This liberal policy had the desired effect of encouraging Jewish enterprise in many directions: while the older settlers remained on their extensive plantations, the new arrivals went into commerce rather than agriculture. Some set up profitable businesses as professional translators; others used their knowledge of the Portuguese and Dutch languages to become indispensable middlemen, operating the bulk of retail trade; still others joined the sugar-export business, maintaining close ties with their coreligionists in Amsterdam for that purpose; a few became tobacco merchants, real estate dealers, and mineral prospectors, and there was at least one Jewish engineer, who, in 1640, constructed a bridge in Pernambuco costing 128,000 guilders.

The two main sources of company revenue in Brazil were levies on the output of the sugar mills and duties on the importation of Negro slaves, and in both these spheres Jewish entrepreneurs were active. In 1638, for example, Monses Navarro bought the right to "farm" the tax on sugar from the Pernambuco district for fifty-four thousand guilders. Jewish speculators bought slaves for ready cash from the Dutch West India Company and resold them to the planters at three or four times the purchase price, since they had to accept payment by installments and often in kind. (Although this is not the place to recount the miserable working conditions of the African slaves in seventeenth-century Brazil, those sold to Jewish planters seem to have been somewhat better off than the ones purchased by Portuguese or Dutch colonists, since they not only rested on the Jewish Sabbath but also— by statute—on Sunday.)

The prosperous state of Brazilian Jewry at this time was commented on by many visitors, such as the Dutch traveler Nieuhof, who roamed through the territory during the 1640s and later reported: "Among the free inhabitants [*vrijluiden*] of Brazil that were not in the company's service, those of the Jewish nation were the most considerable in number, many of whom had transplanted themselves thither from Holland. For the most part, they concerned themselves with business, having a vast traffic beyond the rest; they operated numerous sugar mills, and in Recife [Pernambuco] built stately houses" (Johan Nieuhof, *Gedenkweerdige Brasiliaense Zee -en Lant Reize* [Amsterdam, 1682], p. 214).

Signs of resentment toward this prosperity were soon forthcoming from the Christian colonists: in December 1637 some of the old Portuguese settlers petitioned the company to expel the Jews, or, if that was not feasible, at least to prohibit them from all retail trade. And in 1641, in a letter to Governor Maurits, sixty-six Christian merchants protested that in recent years shiploads of poor Jews came to the colony, where they enriched themselves at the Christians' expense, since the wealthy Jewish residents who controlled the sugar trade gave all the best positions to these newly arrived coreligionists.

Maurits turned a deaf ear to this and similar anti-Semitic outbursts, and when they heard the news of the governor's imminent return to Holland, the Jews entreated the Heeren XIX (the company's board of directors) "that if His Excellency could be paid to stay in this land by the purchase of anything in the world, that they would find no price too great to pay, even if it were their own blood, if only they might retain him." Maurits was approached directly by a small group of wealthy Jewish planters and sugar traders and offered a yearly stipend of three thousand guilders to remain in the colony; but in May 1644 this capable and tolerant administrator left the New World, and almost immediately thereafter the power of the Dutch company in Brazil began to wane.

After sixty years of uneasy political union with their Iberian cousins, the Portuguese had proclaimed their independence from Spain in 1640. It was a step that made the future status of Brazil extremely uncertain, and the company directors became reluctant to invest in long-term development projects in case the captured provinces reverted to Portugal. This policy of retrenchment was fully exploited by Portuguese agents, who proceeded to stir up anti-Dutch feelings among the older colonists and the local tribes.

The Jewish community did everything possible to check such agitation against the company, since it fully realized that if Portuguese control was reestablished its own religious and economic privileges would be gravely curtailed, if not swept away altogether. But the situation began to deteriorate rapidly after Pernambuco (with its sizable Jewish community of some one thousand) was besieged toward the end of 1645. For more than six years the beleaguered town remained obdurate, despite getting little assistance from the company and having to endure increasing hardship. Some indication of the economic plight of the Jews during these years is provided by the case of Jorgo Homen Pinto, formerly one of the settlement's wealthiest planters and the owner of 370 slaves and nine sugar mills, who now found himself in debt to the tune of almost 1 million guilders. When the company became embroiled in the Anglo-Dutch War (1652), it was able to do even less in support of its Brazilian enterprise, and by 1654 it had been completely ousted from the territory.

On occupying Pernambuco, the Portuguese commander, General Barreto (according to one contemporary chronicler), "prohibited any person of the Hebrew nation from being touched or molested, and provided severe penalties against those acting contrary to this prohibition" (Saul Levy Mortera, "Providencia de Dios con Ysrael . . . ," translated in Arnold Wiznitzer, "The Number of Jews in Dutch Brazil, 1630–1654," *Jewish Social Studies* 16 [1954]: 112–13). Yet since the surrender terms contained the ominous clause "Jews and other non-Catholics shall receive the same treatment as in Portugal," it is not surprising that at least six hundred of the more recent immigrants took advantage of Barreto's permission to sell their properties and merchandise and return to Holland. At least an equal number left for the West Indies, while one shipload eventually reached New Amsterdam—the Dutch West India Company's settlement on the Hudson—thus becoming "the Jewish Pilgrim fathers" of North America.

Several hundred Jews must have remained in the colony after the reconquest, however, since the Brazil Company (founded by the Portuguese in 1649 to take over the trade of the Dutch West India Company) was subsequently able to impose forced loans on "New Christian" merchants in Bahia and Pernambuco; and when the activities of several prominent traders in Rio de Janeiro were temporarily suspended by the officers of the Inquisition in the early eighteenth century, work on the neighboring mines and plantations was so gravely dislocated that "production and commerce of the province required a long stretch of time to recover from the blow." Yet although these Marrano remnants remained important to the Brazilian economy, they gradually assimilated with the general population (it was only after 1823, when Brazil declared its independence and liberty of worship was proclaimed, that fresh immigration restored Jewish communal life).

The restoration of Portuguese power in Brazil in the mid-seventeenth century, by promoting a large-scale Jewish exodus, ultimately resulted in a serious contraction of the colony's economy. The Jewish refugees who settled in the Caribbean islands owned by the Dutch, French, and English brought with them their knowledge of sugar culture, established thriving plantations, and introduced the techniques of drying and crystallizing the extracted cane juices. As a consequence, the exports of the West Indies increased by leaps and bounds, until by the early eighteenth century Brazilian sugar had virtually been eliminated from the markets of Europe by this competition.

22

THE MAINSPRING OF
AMERICAN JEWISH
ENTERPRISE

Overawed by the sheer size of American Jewry—a community now close to the 6-million mark—we are apt to forget that in 1860 there were only an estimated 150,000 Jews in the whole United States. But an awareness of such recent origins renders the socioeconomic achievements of American Jewry all the more impressive.

Two fundamental factors can be said to have shaped the socioeconomic character of Jewish life in the United States: the traditions that the immigrants brought with them across the Atlantic and the economic evolution of the United States itself during the period of mass Jewish immigration.

No group of newcomers arrives in a country quite empty-handed. Though it may bring little in the way of material possessions, it does bring with it certain traditions, habits, perhaps even some specialized skills. It is true that the immigrants' own position in the new society ultimately will be determined by the stage and tempo of economic development within the new environment itself; but it is equally true that various ethnic groups, each with their own socioeconomic heritages, are differently prepared and suited for the utilization of the new conditions and for making adjustments to promote their own development.

Throughout the second half of the nineteenth century immigrants were drawn to the United States from many lands —some of them from very backward agrarian communities. But the forebears of the Jews among them (those from Poland, the Balkans, the Baltic countries, and Russia) had been urban for many centuries. And it is a matter of common historical observation that a townsman is usually quicker to reorient himself to new conditions, learn a new language, and recognize the potential opportunities available in a new environment than is a country-dweller, who is accustomed to a static situation of rural self-sufficiency and very often to the impediments of serfdom. And this contrast was particularly true of the Jews in relation to the non-Jews of the backward lands of Central and Eastern Europe; because of their urban background they were bound to be more enterprising, more adaptable, and more resilient than non-Jewish immigrants from the same regions.

Mass migration began in the early 1880s, bringing about 1.5 million Jews from Russia and Russian-occupied territories in less than thirty years. It was a movement that did not result solely from anti-Jewish persecution, although pogroms frequently provided the last prod to emigration. But during this same period (about 1880–1910) there also was a great Jewish exodus from Austro-Hungary (about 300,000 immigrants came to the United States from the district of Galicia alone, although there were no pogroms in that region); the same decades also witnessed a great spurt in non-Jewish immigration from Eastern and Central Europe. In fact, rapid population growth, protracted commercial depression, and the positive stimulus provided by the advent of cheap rail and steamship passages induced Jews and non-Jews alike to seek new homes.

In each decade after 1880 the number of newcomers was

almost equal to the total Jewish population in America at the beginning of the decade, and in the big cities they soon constituted a majority. The number of Jews in New York in 1881 has been estimated at 75,000 (mainly of Sephardic and German origins); ten years later that city held more than 250,000 Jews, of whom about 150,000 were concentrated on the East Side, from the Bowery up to Fourteenth Street.

Contrary to popular opinion, the flow continued over the four decades after World War I, between 1920 and 1960, though at a reduced rate; in the course of these forty years some 700,000 Jews arrived in the United States (of whom more than 50 percent came from Eastern Europe). To these should be added a few tens of thousands who entered via Canada, Mexico, and Cuba, having gone first to those countries to circumvent the quota limitations that had been introduced in 1921.

All these figures are far from exact, for it was only between 1899 and 1943 that the authorities classified Jews as a separate immigrant group (in the latter year, at the height of the Nazi massacres, the term "Hebrew" was finally deleted from the official entry forms). Thus for almost half the time since 1880 we have to rely on estimates. But there can be no denying the vast scale of Jewish immigration into the United States, especially from Eastern Europe.

The first big wave of immigrants consisted primarily of unskilled manual workers and youths who had just left the cheder or yeshivah with no experience or training for earning a livelihood. Unlike the majority of non-Jewish immigrants from the same regions, they were not the children of peasants but the sons of storekeepers, peddlers, and people of no fixed economic class who still lived in the atmosphere of the traditional Jewish hamlet, with its synagogues, study houses, and communal assistance.

The second large wave of Jewish immigrants (from 1900 to 1925) for the most part comprised artisans and skilled workers, more than two-thirds of whom had been engaged as tailors, cap- and hat-makers, and carpenters. Many of them had participated in the antitsarist revolutionary movements in Russia and Poland and brought with them progressive social ideas. Unafraid of authority and more imaginative than the average newcomer, they carried their dynamic energy over into private business enterprise on the other side of the Atlantic.

Former talmudic students, teachers, would-be intellectuals and political reformers, petty merchants and craftsmen, now—on the soil of the New World—became cutters, cloak-makers, and peddlers. Undisciplined, highly individualistic, they were also more alert, more restless, and more impatient than the average non-Jewish immigrant.

However, such traits by themselves are not sufficient to enable an ethnic group to utilize fully its experiences and skills in a new land. Fortunately, from 1880 to 1940—the main decades of Jewish immigration—almost ideal objective conditions prevailed in the United States to encourage the maximum application of these accumulated energies.

Agriculture—formerly the most important branch of American economic activity—increased only one-sixth as fast as the population in general during this period. Moreover, the proportion of people engaged in the heavy capital-goods industries remained almost static (27 percent in 1880, 26 percent in 1940). But in the service and distribution branches of American economic life it was a different story; the number of persons engaged in light consumer-goods industries, commerce, and white-collar occupations (including the learned professions) increased more than twelvefold over these sixty years.

The enormous growth of an urban population, accom-

Peddlers on Hester Street, New York City, early 1900s; courtesy of
Library of Congress

panied by an ever-increasing demand for those goods and services which in Central and Eastern Europe had been traditionally in Jewish hands (that is, the production and distribution of consumer articles and certain of the professions), presented exceedingly favorable opportunities for the new immigrants, with their centuries-old experience in these fields.

By the beginning of the present century a small handful of these newcomers, with traditional Jewish perseverance, had managed to study medicine or law at night school, after a hard day's work, and had climbed several rungs of the economic ladder. But they were the exception rather than the rule, and in general the Jewish population of the United States at that time consisted primarily of manual workers.

Today Jews constitute about 28 percent of the population of the city of New York—their largest urban concentration in the U.S.; but in some of the economic activities of that city Jewish participation is proportionately very much higher. It is especially high in goods designed for mass consumption: about 50 percent of New York's wholesale and 65 percent of its retail stores are Jewish-owned; in certain trades this proportion is even greater—over 80 percent of all clothing shops are run by Jews and most of the employees in such shops are Jewish; the proportions for furniture and food stores are almost as high.

As far as the light industries of New York are concerned, over 90 percent of the city's furriers are Jews, 85 percent of the textile factories are Jewish-owned (though only 50 percent of the labor force employed by them is Jewish), while glassware, paper, and plastic products are all high up on the list. As regards Jewish participation in the professions, it has been estimated that 65 percent of New York City's lawyers, approximately 60 percent of its physicians and dentists, 55 percent of its musicians and music teachers, about half of its professional artists and actors, and more than 40 percent of its journalists are Jews.

Nor, it would seem, is this pattern of occupation distribution confined to the big cities. For example, in Stamford, Connecticut, a small industrial town where Jews constitute only 5 percent of the population, it was found that over 80 percent of the clothing shops, all the large delicatessen and food stores, 85 percent of the jewelry shops, and 60 percent of the furniture and electrical appliance shops were run by Jewish businessmen.

One final but quite significant statistical observation, which probably has wider application: a survey of the Jewish population of Detroit (which numbers seventy-five thousand) indicated that wage and salary earners totaled something like 60 percent of all Jews in that city who were gainfully employed (which is about one-quarter less than the proportion for the general community), and within this group not more than 25 percent could be classified as manual workers.

These figures may not be very exact. (Unfortunately, no official statistics exist on the occupational distribution of the present-day American Jews; the census forms do not contain any questions on nationality or religion. But the available data, which are based on private investigations generally sponsored by various Jewish bodies, are sufficient for the purpose despite their limitations.) Viewed in the perspective of history, however, they show that the quantitative growth of American Jewry has been accompanied by a qualitative expansion in its contribution to the economy of the United States.

23

THE JEWISH IMPACT
ON SOUTH AFRICAN
ECONOMIC DEVELOPMENT

It is always difficult to assess the specific contributions to
economic progress made by particular ethnic groups in
heterogeneous societies. The case of the South African Jewish community presents its own particular problems of evalu-
ation: relatively little of the factual material needed for ex-
tracting and interpreting basic trends is to be found in those
happy hunting grounds of economic historians, the Blue
Book and the commission report. Instead, much of the essential information has to be sifted from neglected newspaper
files, forgotten family letters, and the recollections of surviving pioneer settlers, whose reminiscences are inevitably colored and distorted by the passage of time. It is hardly surprising, therefore, that most of the works dealing with various
aspects of the history of the Jews in South Africa have
adopted an anecdotal approach, emphasizing the activities of
those individuals who made their mark on Jewish communal
affairs but hardly touching on the general factors that have
enabled this community to play a role of some significance in
the evolution of the contemporary South African scene.

In the middle decades of the nineteenth century the great
bulk of the Jewish people still lived in provincial townships

and hamlets under tsarist or Turkish rule. It was an unprivileged ghetto existence of cultural isolation and perpetual economic hardship, with most of these communities just paying their way by petty shopkeeping and small-scale trading activities. Neither of the two prime forces then at work in the West—the growth of personal liberty and the rapid mechanization of economic life—had as yet exerted any major influence on these static Jewries of Eastern Europe and Asia Minor.

At the same time, however, the advent of the railway and the steamship had set in motion a great outward movement of peoples from the Continent as a whole, and during the peak period of this migration (about 1870–1910), when more than 1 million emigrants were leaving Europe annually to establish homes abroad, the percentage of Jewish emigrants was much higher than that of any other ethnic group. After centuries of precarious existence as an alien urban people among deeply rooted peasant communities, they now sought freer environments in which their traditional occupations would have more valuable outlets. It was a movement that radically altered the distribution of the world's Jewish population, and while the mainstream of emigration was across the North Atlantic to the United States, important settlements were also established elsewhere, of which the rise of a substantial South African Jewish community was among the most significant.

The majority of the forty thousand Jewish settlers who reached the shores of southern Africa during these years came from the Russian-controlled territory of Lithuania—a land that, in common with the other Baltic dominions of the tsar, was still unaffected by large-scale industrialization and suffered from relative overpopulation and from those periodic catastrophes of flood, fire, and cholera which the Western lands had brought under control many centuries earlier.

Moreover, the region's Jewish community of some 250,000 was subject to a restricted area of settlement, arbitrary deportation, discriminatory educational and conscription laws, and (after the assassination of Alexander II in 1881) widespread pogroms, as the Russians tried to divert public attention from their autocratic regime. Consequently, when favorable opportunities presented themselves, there was no lack of motives for emigration.

Rather less obvious are the reasons why these Lithuanian Jews displayed such a preference for settling in South Africa when so many of their coreligionists from other parts of Central and Eastern Europe were streaming to America. A handful of Lithuanian Jews had found their way to South Africa during the 1860s, after having been stranded in England because of some difficulty about their passage to the United States. Most of these fortuitous immigrants were soon firmly established in the Cape Colony or Transvaal, and the contents of their letters home quickly became common knowledge in such a close-knit community. So when the mass exodus of the eighties began, relatives and friends had had plenty of opportunity to learn something of the possibilities that South Africa offered to prospective settlers. Furthermore, a number of these pioneers were soon returning to their native towns on visits or to collect their families, and were able to report in person about the unlimited freedom and economic opportunities prevailing in these seemingly remote parts.

Although every mass migration has its quota of restless spirits who leave the homeland to satisfy a love of adventure or a longing for fabulous wealth, it is usually the general economic background that is the determining factor. While many of the Polish and German Jews had already become factory workers and, having lived in a capitalistic environment, could fairly easily adapt to the garment workshops of

New York, the Jews of Lithuania were shopkeepers, itinerant peddlers, or petty craftsmen who labored in their own small workshops. It was only natural, therefore, that the latter should prefer the greater economic independence that South African settlement offered to those who were not wage earners.

The movement was not so very different in character from the spasmodic immigration of British settlers into South Africa over the same decades: the men would go first and, once established, would be joined by wives (actual or prospective), children, aged parents, and, in due course, by relations who were less close. It was a cumulative family affair.

Although it was only during and after the early diamond and gold rushes that Jewish mass immigration began to exercise a pronounced effect on South African economic life, the activities of the pioneer settlers in the middle decades of the nineteenth century reveal that a specifically Jewish influence on the pulse of development was already being felt and indicate the nature of the initial problems that had to be surmounted. Much of the early correspondence from South Africa published in the Hebrew press of Eastern Europe did not describe a land flowing with milk and honey, but stressed, rather, the hazards and dislocations of pioneering life where both British colonies and Boer republics were beset by trade recessions, droughts, floods, and tribal wars.

Yet it was a country in which (as one writer put it) "there is no discrimination between a Hebrew and a Christian. Every man attends to his labors diligently and finds a reward for his toil. Most of our brethren who come there by the skin of their teeth, naked as on the day of their birth, are being shown mercy by the existing Jewish settlers the moment they put their foot on the shores of Africa. With the help of this generosity they acquire a few pounds' worth of goods and little trinkets and they begin to trudge round the towns and villages with their merchandise. . . . After they save a little sum they turn from peddling-on-back to trading on a bigger scale, traveling in wagons drawn by ten oxen" (quoted in Gus Saron and Louis Hotz, eds., *The Jews in South Africa: A History* [New York, 1955], pp. 70–71).

And apparently the customers of these early traders were finding that they performed a much-neglected function, for when the question of the "peddler Jew" was raised in the Cape legislature, one speaker said: "The proper way of dealing with these people is for farmers to warn them off their land. But the extraordinary thing I find is that the farmers encourage these men and the farmers' wives and daughters are their customers" (quoted in Saron and Hotz, op. cit., p. 87).

A country in which slavery had only recently been done away with and where many members of the small white community had grown up with a tradition of contempt for manual labor offered tremendous scope to these active newcomers, who, far from being work-shy, displayed a remarkable aptitude for quickly adapting themselves to a strange environment and did not look upon any lawful task as being below their dignity if they saw in it a chance to improve their position.

Meanwhile, the original Jewish immigrants—mostly from Germany and England—were already firmly established, and by the middle of the century many of them had progressed from the initial hawking stage to the ownership of shops and warehouses. Through these premises flowed a considerable share of the thin stream of commerce that sufficed for a sparsely populated and predominantly self-sufficient country.

A few of these pioneers had advanced very much further, like the Mosenthal brothers, who, during the forties and fifties, had established a series of trading stations in the central and eastern Cape which became entrepôts for the marketing of merino fleeces and mohair; their unofficial banknotes (at a time when there were few commercial banks in the colony) enjoyed unquestioned confidence and were freely negotiable. Other such success stories were those of the De Pass family, with their ambitious whaling and seal-oil factories along the west coast, their ship-repairing yards in Table Bay, and their introduction of cold storage; and Jonas Bergtheil, with his elaborate Natal Cotton Company (which turned out to be a commercial failure but served as an initial stimulant to European immigration into Natal). These are merely the more striking examples "of the Jewish pioneering spirit thrusting forward into unknown or untried economic fields in the new land and helping, often with conspicuous success, to mould the future of South Africa" (Saron and Hotz, op. cit., p. 353).

The nature of this "pioneering spirit" becomes clearer if one considers the Jewish contribution to the successful exploitation of the great mineral wealth discovered on the High Veld. Not only were Jews prominent among the original prospectors along the river diggings and at Kimberley, but also most of the early miners' stores and hotels were Jewish-owned; and a Jewish syndicate established the first regular passenger coach service, operating a team of wagons between the diamond fields and the coast. Furthermore, the researches of a Danish-born Jewish scientist, Dr. Emil Cohen —who subsequently became a professor of geology at the University of Strasbourg—provided the first acceptable account of the rock structure of Griqualand West and of the geological origins of the dry diggings. Most significant of all, however, the actual marketing of the stones was mainly in the hands of a small group of German Jews with an expert knowledge of the world gem trade. Operating at first as individual dealers and brokers, they had soon formed imposing syndicates, thereby stabilizing a highly speculative activity. They were now in a position to consign considerable quantities of stones to European and British buyers, making advances to the miners to tide them over until they were paid.

After the main gold deposits on the Witwatersrand were opened up in 1886, many of the Jewish pioneers, who had played a notable role in establishing the diamond industry, switched their attentions to the southern Transvaal—but by that time local Jews had taken an active part in the discovery and leasing of some of the major reefs and had been responsible, in the winter of 1885, for introducing the first quartz-crushing machinery to the new fields.

The "mining revolution" was a product of many complex factors, and while Jewish enterprise was certainly one of these, it is extremely unlikely that its influence in those decades was decisive. A much more valid case can be made for a distinctive Jewish contribution to economic development during the first half of the twentieth century.

Although the mineral discoveries had provided an impetus for secondary production, at the time that the Union of South Africa was formed (1910) fewer than 100,000 workers were employed in manufacturing; large factories were still extremely rare. Labor, though plentiful, was untrained and inefficient (which meant, too, that the purchasing power of the domestic market was very limited), there was a good deal of prejudice—much of it justified—against "colonial" goods, and the bulk of the country's manufactured products came from overseas.

Of the four ethnic groups that might have been expected to play prominent parts in promoting further industrialization at that time, the Jews were most favorably placed. For

centuries the Afrikaners had lived in an environment of economic self-sufficiency in which virtually all manual work was
done by various groups of nonwhite labor. With their close
attachment to the land, few Afrikaners at the time of union
were anxious to perform humble, routine jobs in embryo
factories, training Coloured and Bantu personnel in the techniques of the new machine age. While dislike for "kaffir (native) work" kept the Afrikaners out of industry, the settlers
of English origin tended to retain close commercial ties with
"home"; as businessmen they preferred to meet local needs
by importing from Britain rather than by undertaking the
considerable risks of manufacturing on their own account.
The hardworking and resourceful Indian community of Natal, with a business acumen no less finely developed than its
counterparts in tropical East Africa, was nevertheless prevented from becoming industrially significant by various political and legal devices restricting its entrepreneurial activities.

On the other hand, the forty thousand Jewish immigrants
who had arrived during the three decades before union enjoyed full freedom of enterprise, which had been denied to
them in Eastern Europe. Many of them had begun their new
lives as itinerant traders, gaining an intimate knowledge of
the country and its human and material resources as they
moved across the veld with a peddler's pack or a trader's
wagon. They came to know where industrially useful raw
materials were located and were soon familiar with the marketing prospects for goods that could be fashioned from such
materials.

Nor did these potential Jewish industrialists require very
much capital to commence operations. Before heavy industries (like steel-processing plants) could be set up, light articles for direct consumption first had to appear on the scene.
(This familiar chronology in the pattern of capitalistic devel-

222 / ASPECTS OF JEWISH ECONOMIC HISTORY

opment has only been reversed by the state-sponsored industries of the Communist world—and then not always successfully.) If the individual's own small savings from petty trading
were inadequate, the very strong family ties prevailing in the
new community would induce friends and relations to invest
in a likely project. Any shortfall that still remained could be
bridged by negotiating favorable credit terms through the
business contacts already established in town and countryside.

So it was that a combination of negative and positive circumstances made the Jew well qualified to set the new political union on its industrial feet.

Once the Jewish entrepreneur had accumulated sufficient
resources and know-how to switch from trade to industry, he
was aided in his efforts by the impact of World War I: profits
were inflated by a general price level that rose more rapidly
than costs of production, overseas shipping services were
disrupted, and gaps in the range of consumer goods had to
be filled. Haltingly, and often with much difficulty in make-
shift workshops on the Rand and in the coastal cities of Cape
Town and Port Elizabeth, he began to turn out textiles and
blankets, furniture and glassware, processed foods and con-
fectionery, tobacco products, and a host of other consumer
items. Only in the Durban area did Jewish industrialists remain inactive, for there they had been unable to compete
with Indian traders and were in no position to turn to manufacturing; until British firms began investing capital, South
Africa's largest port lagged behind as a hub of secondary
industry.

The Great Depression in 1929–30 brought worldwide
unemployment in its wake, and conditions could seldom
have been more favorable for the ambitious political adven-
turer with the skill to manipulate economic discontent.

South Africa emerged from the crisis relatively unscathed, especially after the international currency disturbances of 1932 had led to an increase in the price of gold. Central Europe was less fortunate, and as German Jewish emigrants fled the Hitler terror, some of them brought to South African shores special aptitudes that served to expand greatly the range of industrial pursuits—particularly in the spheres of fashion, ceramics, diamond cutting, and jewelry.

By the time World War II broke out some Jewish-owned industrial units had become large corporations, with a trend toward vertical integration and a growing use of assembly-plant methods. The new world struggle stimulated local heavy industry, and soon Jews were manufacturing agricultural machinery and electrical equipment, while others were breaking completely new ground (as in paints and plastics), promoting technical research, and seeking wider markets for their products, especially in the Rhodesias.

Precise data on these developments are tantalizingly scant. Yet it is not unreasonable to infer that the industrial revolution in South Africa stemmed in no small measure from Jewish entrepreneurial initiative.

Having helped to promote a new urban factory civilization at the southern tip of the "dark continent," Jewish energy also aided the countryside to keep pace. Jewish farmers became prominent in the scientific production and mass marketing of maize, potatoes, honey, citrus and other fruits, and commercial farming in general owed much to their enterprise.

Although such agricultural innovations were the work of a small group, the Jewish role in commerce was both qualitatively and quantitatively significant; many an itinerant peddler became a sedentary shopkeeper, while the more successful emerged as wholesale distributors or set up imposing trading houses. A distinctive Jewish innovation was the multiple chain store (or "bazaar") type of business, which gave the poorer elements of the population access to cheap, mass-produced products of every kind.

Nor did the Jew in South Africa confine his activities to the production and distribution of goods. He also established a special niche for himself in the provision of certain services: medical, legal, and accounting. The hotel, catering, advertising, and entertainment (theater, movies, tourist, sports) businesses as well came to rest very largely on Jewish enterprise.

In spite of its considerable stakes in secondary industry and commerce, South African Jewry has exerted little influence in the sphere of finance. The country's banking, stock exchange, and other specialized financial institutions evolved without much direct Jewish participation—one exception being insurance, where Jews played some (though not an overriding) part in creating adequate facilities for risk-bearing. They participated fully in the organization of representative bodies (there have been Jewish presidents and chairmen of the major chambers of commerce and of the Federated Chamber of Industries) and, as editors of technical and commercial journals, in the dissemination of knowledge.

A less obvious but probably more significant contribution was the manner in which Jewish businessmen in shops and factories voluntarily assumed social responsibilities that, for the time and place, were innovations. The provision of rest rooms and canteen facilities, adequate ventilation and lighting, free medical attention, savings plans—these and other welfare aids benefited European and African employees long before such improvements in working conditions became statutory obligations. The people of the Book had not forgotten the injunction in the Book of Job (31: 13–15) to treat their workmen with justice and humanity.

*   *   *

White South Africa has now reached an age of high mass consumption; "poor whitism" is no longer a pressing problem, and the majority of the 4 million whites are now enjoying consumption standards that compare favorably with those in many parts of the Western world.

For the country's 18 million nonwhites the picture is very different, and there remains a tremendous need to improve their productivity, their earning powers, and their living conditions. To the extent that current ideologies and official policies permit fresh economic advancement, South African Jewry is well placed to play a prominent part in the process of further social uplift.

Taking the long-term view, however, the significance of a specifically Jewish contribution is likely to experience a relative decline. To refer to a *Jewish impact* on development during the previous century is quite legitimate. As indicated above, the Jews as a group possessed certain aptitudes that their neighbors either had not yet acquired or were prevented from using to the full.

That situation has now altered radically: the Afrikaners are fast becoming urbanized and even in the country districts are taking a growing interest in nonagricultural activities; for the most part, settlers of British origin have severed their economic ties with "home"; the nonwhites are no longer confined to purely unskilled manual jobs; and the Jews themselves are expending their energies over a wider and wider field. Thus, while many individual Jewish businessmen will undoubtedly continue to make their mark, South African Jewry as a group will probably merge into an increasingly variegated productive pattern based on further mechanization and specialization.

24

ISRAEL'S
ECONOMIC REBIRTH

Jewish history has been perennial drama, sometimes comic in the Aristotelian sense of having a happy ending, much more often tragic, and always played to a full house—usually before a hostile audience. In our own times the emergence of a Third Jewish Commonwealth stands as a counterforce to the Holocaust in this ongoing tragicomedy.

Perhaps the most distinctive and decisive feature of Israel's economic development during its first quarter century of life was population increase. More people came to the country between 1948 and 1973 than during the preceding eighty years of Jewish settlement, and the state's Jewish population grew from less than 650,000 to nearly 3 million. Today the majority of inhabitants is made up not of those who fought and worked for the establishment of Israel but of newcomers and those born since the War of Independence.

Of course, a mere quantitative increase of this nature is not in itself a sufficient guarantee of economic progress. The qualities of the people—especially when contrasted with those of their immediate neighbors—have been equally significant. Four elements in particular favored growth: a high rate of literacy, the presence of a well-educated elite, a strong sense of social justice, and effective administrative machinery (certainly by Middle Eastern standards).

Since its birth, economically speaking, Israel has to its credit handsome achievements against great odds. On the international league table of growth Israel's rate of development was second only to Japan's—an average annual upswing of 10 percent in real terms. This was an achievement by a country which, like Japan (or Sweden or Switzerland, for that matter), was strikingly unendowed with natural resources: few minerals to speak of, insufficient water, and not much space.

Unlike those other countries, Israel has had to face an increasingly heavy defense burden to ward off the continual threats to its very existence from Arab neighbors. On the other hand, each of the four wars fought against these enemies between 1948 and 1973, while causing short-term distortions, also promoted economic growth in a number of significant directions (such as the rise of a sophisticated electronics sector as a result of the need for self-sufficiency in certain advanced types of defense equipment).

Until the foundation of the state, the Jewish community of Palestine could claim with a good deal of justification that it was a classless society (at any rate, in the economic sense). The reasons for this are not hard to find, for the development of the area that was to become the state of Israel followed a course unique in the history of modern colonization.

From the outset of Zionist activities in the country, development projects in both agriculture and industry had for the most part been communal efforts; labor had organized itself into a powerful trade union movement before the arrival of pioneers with capital; most attempts to employ cheap Arab workers—and so undermine the foundations of the embryo socialist state—had been frustrated by the 1930s (so that no

Top: *Biluim*, first Zionist settlers, having dinner in field, early 1900s; courtesy Zionist Archives and Library

Bottom: scene on banks of Jordan, Deganiah ("mother of *kvutzot*"), c. 1925; courtesy Zionist Archives and Library

significant landlord class survived); and above all there loomed the dominant ideology that manual labor under these circumstances was more valuable than intellectual abilities.

But once the state had been launched and mass immigration got under way, it soon became apparent that this classless society had been the product of very special social and economic circumstances. The pre-1948 community had formed a highly cohesive group, most of whose members were idealists accepting great austerity for the present as a means toward ultimately making a decent living from neglected soil. The classic Zionist philosophy of transforming colonists into a compact society of workers carried with it the tacit implication that one became such a worker by free choice and by diligent effort, and that the economy itself would remain a relatively simple and a predominantly agrarian one.

In the face of the increasingly complex economic and social realities of Israel as it has evolved since 1948, this ideology has become progressively outmoded.

The diversification of Israel's economy following statehood and the phenomenon of mass immigration (which tripled the population in just over a decade) inevitably resulted in the creation of a technological hierarchy; that is to say, as agriculture and other primary occupations like fishing and mining, together with secondary industry, spread out in new directions, both mechanization and specialization became much more pronounced, so that distinct categories of skilled, semiskilled, and unskilled workers emerged.

Moreover, the government's decision during the very early years of statehood to create a "mixed economy" that would include both publicly owned and private sectors, and to grant state assistance to encourage private investment in commerce and in industry, created the paradoxical situation of a socialist government promoting the emergence of a private enterprise entrepreneurial class.

Meanwhile, the dynamics of mass immigration had generated boom conditions that were further fueled by assistance from Jewish communities abroad as well as by German reparations. Under these circumstances all sorts of inflationary pressures forced prices upward; wages spiraled in their wake and then took the lead as productivity itself increased.

But this rising wave of material prosperity by no means washed over the whole community. Most of the principal benefits of enhanced living standards were reaped by the veterans of the prestate society (now very much of a numerical minority), while the newcomers seemed destined to become a working class in the traditional sense of that term—though the term itself has been somewhat tarnished by the impact of Marxian economics.

This situation had arisen not because of any discrimination against the newcomers but simply because the immigrants themselves were not equipped to play a fuller part in an economic miracle—a miracle which in the obstacles it had to surmount far outstripped anything achieved in West Germany or Japan during the same years of the immediate postwar era.

Most of the immigrants who arrived after the foundation of the of the state came as penniless refugees, either from the shambles and ashes of postwar Europe or from the Muslim countries of North Africa and the Middle East. All were entitled to the same welfare benefits, and both housing and employment were provided without distinction. But their background, education and training, and, frequently, reparation compensations helped those of European origin to gain ground very much more rapidly.

Though today the difference between the higher and lower income groups in Israel is still one of the smallest in the

King Solomon's copper mines in Negev, 1953; courtesy Zionist Archives and Library

world, and though most of the new immigrants have certainly improved their economic position by settling in Israel, the uncomfortable fact is that the division between the more prosperous and the poorer citizens of the Third Jewish Commonwealth is also an ethnic division between the Zionist pioneers (and their native-born children), who fill the professional, technical, and administrative positions in the new society, and the later arrivals from Africa and Asia, who for the most part are occupied in unskilled manual tasks in urban industry and in agriculture.

Having fallen somewhat into the error which modern economic planners frequently make—that of regarding labor as an abstract factor of production and neglecting its very real human aspects—the Israel government seems to be increasingly aware of these inequalities and is beginning to place greater emphasis on restoring equality of opportunity through extending and raising the educational facilities available to the more recent arrivals.

The economic history of modern Israel is very much the story of pioneers who dared to reformulate the implications of the religious and social principles of their forefathers in the light of the challenges posed by the needs of the twentieth century. Many of their goals have been realized with a completeness almost unparalleled by any other social or national movement in our times.

The birth pangs of Israel in 1948 gave rise to a sort of golden heroic age during these last twenty-seven years. They stimulated the people of the Jewish state to rise to the heights of creative pioneering endeavor under an energetic leadership which, in spite of party divisions, a critical opposition, and the shortcomings of an inexperienced administration, enjoyed the nation's confidence on major issues of public policy and commanded the devotion of thousands of public servants who regarded their work not merely as a job but very often as some sort of sacred mission. This heroic atmosphere has not been conducive to a careful calculation of costs and benefits, a sober appreciation of profit and loss, of economic advantage and disadvantage.

This heroic age is drawing to a close. The edifice having been erected, it is now becoming clear that different qualities are going to be needed to establish and maintain it: more scientific know-how and less pioneering energy, more economic efficiency and less unplanned development. Many old habits and customs will have to be reconsidered and revised. Can there be any doubt that the people of Israel, like their enterprising forebears, will prove equal to the economic challenges that lie ahead?

SELECTED
BIBLIOGRAPHY

No reader concerned with the broad sweep of Jewish economic history can do without Salo W. Baron's monumental
Social and Religious History of the Jews, 2d ed. (Philadelphia
and New York, 1952–69), in 14 volumes, each with detailed
bibliographical notes; Professor Baron's survey extends from
biblical times to the seventeenth century, but places most
emphasis on the Middle Ages. Of particular importance are
the following sections:

Vol. 1, ch. 8 (which deals with social turmoil in the postbib-
lical era);

Vol. 2, ch. 14 (economic trends and policies under talmudic
influence);

Vol. 4, ch. 22 (economic changes in European Jewry during
the High Middle Ages);

Vol. 9, ch. 37 (a discussion of medieval usury);

Vol. 10, ch. 45 (on the decline of Iberian Jewry);

Vol. 12 in its entirety (which deals with the deteriorating
position of European Jewry in the later Middle Ages, examin-
ing closely the role of the Jew as craftsman, merchant,
banker, and taxpayer);

Vol. 13, ch. 56 (on the Marrano dispersion); and

Vol. 14, ch. 62 (on economic policies affecting the Jews of Central Europe during the Thirty Years' War).

ANTIQUITY

The biblical texts referred to in the pieces on economic life in biblical times are the Jewish Publication Society's Holy Scriptures and (for the New Testament) the Revised Standard Version (Thomas Nelson, 1952). E. Heaton, *Everyday Life in Old Testament Times* (London, 1956) is a useful introductory survey, which should be followed by E. Ginzberg, "Studies in the Economics of the Bible," *Jewish Quarterly Review* 22. A great deal of relevant material is to be found in the 4-volume *Interpreter's Dictionary of the Bible* (New York, 1962), especially the articles on agriculture, crafts, debt, inheritance, labor, money, pottery, poverty, ships, trade and commerce, travel and communication, and wages. See also W. F. Albright, *Recent Discoveries in Bible Lands* (London, 1936).

For agriculture in biblical Palestine, see Alfred Bertholet, "Landbau und Altes Testament," *Schweizer Archiv für Volkskunde* 20 (1916); the same author's *History of Hebrew Civilization* (London, 1926) has a chapter on "Trades and Callings" (pp. 194–222); the relevant section (vol. 1, bk. 1, ch. 2) of William Cunningham's *Western Civilization in Its Economic Aspects* (Cambridge, 1923) must be approached with caution. Werner Keller, *The Bible as History* (London, 1956), synthesizes the findings of archeological research and puts forward some plausible theories on the commerce of King Solomon; in *The River Jordan* (Philadelphia, 1946), ch. 5, Nelson Glueck gives an account of how he excavated a complex metal refinery on the site of Ezion-geber; see also I. Mendelsohn, "Guilds in Ancient Palestine," *Bulletin of the American Schools of Oriental Research*, no. 80 (1940).

Max Weber's *Das antike Judentum* (Tübingen, 1921) was

the last volume in a trilogy on the sociology of religion; translated and edited by Hans Gerth and Don Martindale (*Ancient Judaism*, Glencoe, Ill., 1952), it contains a great deal of thought-provoking material on the socioeconomic life of the Hebrews (such as his views on debt remissions in the jubilee year).

For a brief account of economic life during the Pax Romana, see E. T. Salmon, *A History of the Roman World: From 30 B.C. to A.D. 38* (London, 1944), pt. 3, ch. 6. Neither Henri Daniel-Rops, *Daily Life in Palestine at the Time of Christ* (London, 1961), nor Joseph Klausner, *Jesus of Nazareth* (London, 1929), pp. 174–91, nor even the older work by E. Schürer, *A History of the Jewish People in the Time of Jesus Christ* (Edinburgh, 1898), vols. 1 and 2, should be ignored for economic trends in Palestine under the Romans, but a careful scrutiny of Josephus's *Antiquities* and *Wars* (Whiston's translation, republished 1957, Philadelphia) will be more rewarding in many ways. See also A. H. M. Jones, "The Urbanization of Palestine," *Journal of Roman Studies* 21 (1931); A. Büchler, *The Economic Conditions of Judaea after the Destruction of the Second Temple* (London, 1912). The population estimates referred to will be found in J. Beloch, *Die Bevölkerung der griechisch-römischen Welt* (Leipzig, 1886), p. 9; and A. Harnack, *The Mission and Expansion of Christianity in the First Three Centuries* (New York, 1908), 1:3ff. For the Diaspora communities during the Imperial Peace, much information is scattered here and there in the volumes of Tenney Frank, ed., *An Economic Survey of Ancient Rome* (Baltimore, 1938), which should be supplemented by Jean Juster, *Les juifs dans l'Empire romain*, 2 vols. (Paris, 1914); L. Fuchs, *Die Juden Aegyptens in ptolemäischer und römischer Zeit* (Vienna, 1924); and J. Newman, *The Agricultural Life of the Jews in Babylonia 200–500 C.E.* (London, 1932).

THE MEDIEVAL PERIOD

The standard histories on Byzantine Jewry are Samuel Krauss, *Studien zur byzantinisch-jüdischen Geschichte* (Leipzig, 1914), and J. Starr, *The Jews in the Byzantine Empire* (Athens, 1939; republished 1969); the latter (pp. 34–36) puts Byzantium's medieval Jewish population as low as fifteen thousand; A. Andréadès deals specifically with economic activities in "The Jews in the Byzantine Empire," *Economic History* 3 (January 1934), while the organization of silk production and marketing is discussed by R. S. Lopez, "The Silk Industry in the Byzantine Empire," *Speculum* 20 (January 1945), which should be supplemented by ch. 6 of Mark Wischnitzer, *A History of Jewish Crafts and Guilds* (New York, 1965); the remarks of the Fugger agent are reproduced in Jacob R. Marcus, *The Jew in the Medieval World: A Source Book* (Cincinnati, 1938), pp. 412–14.

For the general historical background of Jewish trading activities in the medieval Mediterranean world, see Henri Pirenne, *Mohammed and Charlemagne* (London, 1939). The traffic and trade routes of the Radanites are explored in Louis Rabinowitz, *Jewish Merchant Adventurers* (London, 1948) and J. Brutzkus, "Trade with Eastern Europe, 800–1200," *Economic History Review*, o.s. 13 (1943). On the Italian communities, see Cecil Roth, *The History of the Jews in Italy* (Philadelphia, 1946); O. C. Cox, *The Foundations of Capitalism* (London, 1959); and R. S. Lopez and I. W. Raymond, eds., *Medieval Trade in the Mediterranean World: Illustrative Documents* (London, 1955).

For Islamic Jewry, besides S. D. Goitein's study of the documents of the Cairo geniza, *A Mediterranean Society: Economic Foundations* (Los Angeles, 1967) and his *Letters of Medieval Jewish Traders* (Princeton, 1973), see W. J. Fischel, *The Jews in the Economic and Political Life of Medieval*

Islam (London, 1937). More specialized monographs include L. A. Mayer, *Islamic Metalworkers* (Geneva, 1959) and H. W. Hazard, *The Numismatic History of Late Medieval North Africa* (New York, 1952). See also Jacob Mann's *Jews in Egypt and in Palestine under the Fatimid Caliphs*, 2 vols. (Oxford, 1922) and S. D. Goitein, *Jews and Arabs: Their Contacts through the Ages* (New York, 1964).

The most useful general survey of medieval Roussillon is by Jean-Auguste Brutails, *Étude sur la condition des populations rurales due Roussillon au Moyen Âge* (Paris, 1891). A very detailed economic analysis of extant notarial records forms the basis of R. W. Emery's *Jews of Perpignan in the Thirteenth Century* (New York, 1959). Emery's book should be supplemented by a lengthy series of articles by Pierre Vidal, "Les Juifs dans les anciens comtés de Roussillon et de Cerdagne," *Revue des études juives* 15 (1887): 19–55; 16 (1888): 1–23, 170–203, though Vidal's assessments are somewhat unbalanced, leaning toward the extreme and the bizarre rather than the typical. On the usury problem, see James Parkes, *The Jew in the Medieval Community* (London, 1938), pt. 3.

A detailed study of Jewish urban life in northwestern Europe during the tenth to eleventh centuries, based on the responsa literature, is to be found in Irving A. Agus, *Urban Civilization in Pre-Crusade Europe*, 2 vols. (New York, 1968); Dr. Agus has followed this up with a critical assessment of *The Heroic Age of Franco-German Jewry* (New York, 1969). See also R. S. Lopez, "An Aristocracy of Money in the Early Middle Ages," *Speculum* 28 (1953) and B. D. Weinryb, "The Beginnings of East-European Jewry," in *Studies and Essays in Honor of Abraham A. Neuman* (Philadelphia, 1962).

H. G. Richardson, *The English Jewry under Angevin Kings* (London, 1960), is a full and dispassionate examination of the surviving documents, though it overlooks the important article by P. Elman, "The Economic Causes of the Expulsion of the Jews in 1290," *Economic History Review*, o.s. 7 (1937). Still worth consulting is B. L. Abrahams, *The Expulsion of the Jews from England* (Oxford, 1895), while Joseph Jacobs's collection of documents and records, *The Jews of Angevin England* (London, 1893), remains indispensable.

A. A. Neuman's *Jews in Spain*, 2 vols. (Philadelphia, 1944) has several chapters on economic activities in the Christian kingdoms but little on the expulsion, for the background to which the article by Max Margolis and Alexander Marx remains useful, "The Expulsion of the Jews from Spain," *Jewish Quarterly Review* 20 (1908). William H. Prescott's *History of the Reign of Ferdinand and Isabella*, pt. 1 (originally published in 1837), throws considerable light on the real as well as pretended motives of the fifteenth-century persecutions, about which modern Spanish authors remain unhelpful (see, for instance, Vicens Vives, *An Economic History of Spain* [Princeton, 1969]) and recent British studies factually inaccurate (for example, R. Trevor Davies, *The Golden Century of Spain* [London, 1937], and *Spain in Decline* [London, 1957]). For the operations of the Marranos in Spanish colonial trade, see two books by C. H. Haring, *Trade and Navigation between Spain and the Indies* (Cambridge, Mass., 1918), ch. 5, and *The Spanish Empire in America* (New York, 1947), pp. 203ff.

MERCANTILISM

On the pitfalls attached to the continued use of the concept of mercantilism, see my article "What Do Economic Historians Know? Observations on Some Major Themes," *South African Banker* 66 (November 1969). The standard work on the Marrano dispersion and its repercussions is Cecil Roth's *History of the Marranos* (Philadelphia, 1934). H. I. Bloom's *Economic Activities of the Jews of Amsterdam* (Williamsport, Pa., 1937) is a detailed survey of its subject during the seventeenth and eighteenth centuries, based on a study of archival sources.

D. Patinkin's article on "Mercantilism and the Readmission of the Jews to England," *Jewish Social Studies* 8 (1946), should be read in conjunction with Cecil Roth's "New Light on the Resettlement," *Transactions of the Jewish Historical Society* 11 (1924–27) and his "Resettlement of the Jews in England in 1656," in *Three Centuries of Anglo-Jewish History*, ed. V. D. Lipman (London, 1961), pp. 1–25; see also A. M. Hyamson, *A History of the Jews in England* (London, 1928), chs. 17–20.

There is no useful secondary source on the Jews in early British economic thought: Francis Bacon's views will be found in the World's Classics edition of *The New Atlantis*, pp. 261–63, and James Harrington's in Morley's edition of *The Commonwealth of Oceana* (Cambridge, 1887), pp. 13–14; for William Petty's views, see his *Economic Writings* (ed. Hull, Cambridge, 1899), 1:83–84, 263; Josiah Child's discussion is to be found in his *New Discourse of Trade*, 2d ed. (1690), pp. 141–44; Daniel Defoe makes his comment in *A Tour through England and Wales* (Everyman's Library edition), 2:2–3; for Josiah Tucker, see the selection from his economic writings (ed. Schuyler, New York, 1931), pp. 18–21, 40, 87. On the Jewish origins of both Ricardo and Senior, see Cecil Roth's *Jewish Contribution to Civilization* (London, 1938), ch. 11.

Some aspects of Jewish industrial activities in early modern France are dealt with in J. Decourcelle, *La Condition des juifs de Nice aux 17e et 18e siècles* (Paris, 1923); for the French community's trading activities, see Jonas Weyl, "Les Juifs protégés francais aux échelles du Levant et en Barbarie," *Revue des etudes juives* 12 (1886); M. Bloch, *Les Juifs et la prosperitié publique à travers l'histoire* (Paris, 1889); and Théophile Malvezin, *Histoire des juifs à Bordeaux* (Bordeaux, 1875), pp. 132–75. Antoine de Montchrétien's most important work was *Traicté de l'oeconomie politique* (see, especially, the Funck-Brentano edition [Paris, 1889], pp. 188–93); for Richelieu and Colbert, see C. W. Cole, *Colbert and a Century of French Mercantilism* (New York, 1939), vol. 1.

Further sources on this subject can be found in my article "West European Jewry in the Age of Mercantilism: An Economic Interpretation," *Historia Judaica* 22 (October 1960): 85–104.

SHYLOCK, SOMBART, AND MARX

In addition to Bernard Grebanier's study of *The Merchant of Venice* mentioned in the text (New York, 1962), see the articles by J. W. Draper, "Usury in the Merchant of Venice," *Modern Philology* 33 (August 1935); E. C. Pettet, "The Merchant of Venice and the Problem of Usury," *Essays and Studies* 31 (1945); and B. N. Nelson, "The Usurer and the Merchant Prince," supplement to *The Journal of Economic History* 7 (May 1947). H. W. Farnum's *Shakespeare's Economics* (New Haven, 1931) and R. H. Tawney's introduction to the reprint of Thomas Wilson's *A Discourse upon Usury* (London, 1962) are both highly relevant.

Sombart's *Jews and Modern Capitalism* (Epstein's translation) is now available in a Collier paperback (1962); an incomplete bibliography of Sombart's writings is to be found in M. J. Plotnik, *Werner Sombart and His Type of Economics* (New York, 1937); no complete translation of *Der Moderne Kapitalismus* has yet appeared, but a condensed version has been published by F. L. Nussbaum, under the title *A History of the Economic Institutions of Modern Europe* (New York, 1933). Sombart's detailed arguments against the Weber thesis are to be found in his *Der Bourgeois* (1913), translated by M. Epstein as *The Quintessence of Capitalism* (New York, 1915). The article by Cecil Roth mentioned in the text ("The Economic History of the Jews") appeared in the *Economic History Review* (August 1961).

The text of Marx's essay on Jewish emancipation is given in T. B. Bottomore, ed., *Karl Marx: Early Writings* (London, 1963), pp. 32–40; excerpts from the same essay in a more lively translation are to be found in *A Golden Treasury of Jewish Literature*, ed. L. W. Schwarz (London, 1937), pp. 714–18; the Bauer-Marx controversy is discussed by Sidney Hook, *From Hegel to Marx* (Ann Arbor, 1962; paperback), ch. 3; see also H. P. Adams, *Karl Marx in His Earlier Writings* (London, 1940), ch. 7.

ESSAYS IN BIOGRAPHY

Two important articles on the Goldsmid Brothers are S. R. Cole, "The Goldsmids and the Development of the London Money Market during the Napoleonic Wars," *Economica*, May 1942, and P. H. Emden, "The Brothers Goldsmid and the Financing of the Napoleonic Wars," *Transactions of the Jewish Historical Society* 14 (1935–39). For the general financial background, see R. D. Richards, *Early History of Banking in England* (London, 1929); E. V. Morgan, "Some Aspects of the Bank Restriction Period," *Economic History* (supplement to *Economic Journal*, 1939); and Eli F. Heckscher, *The Continental System* (Oxford, 1922).

On the early Rothschilds, standard references include E. C. Corti, *The Rise of the House of Rothschild, 1770–1830* (London, 1928); Cecil Roth, *The Magnificent Rothschilds* (London, 1939), which contains genealogical tables; and Frederic Morton, *The Rothschilds* (New York, 1962); in addition, see J. T. Flynn, *Men of Wealth* (New York, 1941); R. H. Mottram, *A History of Financial Speculation* (London, 1929); and N. J. Silberling, "Financial and Monetary Policy of Great Britain during the Napoleonic Wars," *Quarterly Journal of Economics* 38 (1924).

There is an entry on David Pacifico in the *Dictionary of*

National Biography, 43:24–25, and an article by A. M. Hyamson, "Don Pacifico," in *Transactions of the Jewish Historical Society* 18 (1953–55); see also J. McCarthy, *A History of Our Own Times,* 11th ed., vol. 2 (London, 1879); L. Sergeant, *Greece in the Nineteenth Century* (London, 1897), ch. 4; and R. W. Seton-Watson, *Britain in Europe, 1789–1914* (Cambridge, 1938).

Until recently little was known of Viscount Bearsted's career because many Shell documents had been lost or destroyed; the void has been handsomely filled by the appearance of *Marcus Samuel, First Viscount Bearsted* (London, 1960) by Robert Henriques, who married Samuel's granddaughter; he is particularly illuminating on the details of the crisis that culminated in the Shell–Royal Dutch merger. Readers not especially interested in the political economy of oil will find between these covers some fascinating sidelights on late Victorian and early Edwardian London and a useful account of British Jewry's changing social status.

A lively account of contemporary trends among British Jewry will be found in Stephen Aris, *The Jews in Business* (London, 1970), which I have summarized in "Jewish Businessmen and the Economic Life of Modern Britain," *Jewish Affairs* (January 1971); see also part 4 of my article "Jewish Ethics and Commercial Life," *Jewish Affairs* (November 1970).

NEW WORLDS

Background information on colonial Brazil will be found in J. P. Calogeras, *A History of Brazil* (Chapel Hill, N.C., 1939), chs. 1–2, though the older account in A. G. Keller, *Colonization* (New York, 1908) is more useful on the purely economic aspects. Much effective use is made of contemporary documents by Arnold Wiznitzer, *Jews in Colonial Brazil* (New York, 1960). The vacillating policy of Manuel I is discussed by

H. V. Livermore, *A History of Portugal* (Cambridge, 1947), ch. 15; conditions on the early sugar plantations are described by Gilberto Freyre, *The Masters and the Slaves* (New York, 1946). Hermann Wätjen, *Das holländische Kolonialreich in Brasilien* (The Hague, 1921) is the standard authority on the period of Dutch intervention, to be supplemented by C. R. Boxer, *The Dutch in Brazil* (Oxford, 1957) (strangely enough, Professor Boxer's recent *The Golden Age of Brazil* [Los Angeles, 1969], which deals with the economic growing pains of colonial Brazil in the first half of the eighteenth century, almost entirely ignores the Jewish influence); on the unresolved problem of the extent of Jewish participation in the Dutch West India Company's activities, see I. G. van Dillen, "Vreemdelingen te Amsterdam in die eerste helft der zeventiende Eeuw—De Portugeesche Joden," *Tijdschrift voor Geschiedenis* (1935), pp. 4–35. The position of the Jewish community after the period of Dutch control is considered by H. I. Bloom, "A Study of Brazilian Jewish History," *Publications of the American Jewish Historical Society* 33 (1934). Population statistics are largely guesses, but see Arnold Wiznitzer, "The Number of Jews in Dutch Brazil," *Jewish Social Studies* 16 (1954).

There is no comprehensive work on Jewish economic life in the United States, but a useful summary of modern trends is to be found in Oscar I. Janowsky, ed., *The American Jew: A Reappraisal* (Philadelphia, 1964), ch. 3 (Nathan Reich, "Economic Status"); see also Nathan Goldberg, *Occupational Patterns of American Jewry* (New York, 1947). The papers by Ellis Rivkin (pp. 23–61) and Allan Tarshish (pp. 263–93), in *Essays in American Jewish History*, ed. Jacob R. Marcus (Cincinnati, 1958), discuss earlier patterns in relation to the favorable climate provided by the spirit of American free enterprise. On the phase of the German community's dominance, see Barry Supple's stimulating article "A Business Elite: German Jewish Finance in Nineteenth Century New York," *Business History Review* (Summer 1957), which is treated on a more popular level by Stephen Birmingham, *Our Crowd: The Great Jewish Families of New York* (New York, 1967).

On the Jewish contribution to South African economic development, there are several useful sections in Gus Saron and Louis Hotz, eds., *The Jews in South Africa: A History* (New York, 1955), which should be supplemented by my article "The Jewish Share in South African Economic Development," *South African Journal of Economics* (June 1956). For some of the earlier pioneers, see my "Jewish Personages in South Africa's Hall of Fame," *Jewish Affairs* (September 1969). Frieda Sichel's *From Refugee to Citizen* (Cape Town, 1966) examines the integration and impact of the German refugees, the economic aspects of which are specifically dealt with in my "German Jewish Refugees in South Africa," *Jewish Affairs* (June 1966); for the era before the mineral discoveries, see Louis Herrman, *A History of the Jews in South Africa* (London, 1930).

The facts and figures of the Jewish state's early economic struggles, with particular emphasis on population growth in relation to productivity trends, are to be found in Don Patinkin, *The Israel Economy: The First Decade* (Jerusalem, 1960); the socioeconomic integration of the Arab minority is discussed by Abner Cohen, *Arab Border-Villages in Israel* (Manchester, England, 1965); the situation just before the Six-Day War is analyzed by David Horowitz, *The Economics of Israel* (Oxford, 1967). A series of articles in *The New Middle East* examine the postwar situation; these include Gideon Levitas, "The Other Israel: Is Poverty the Price of Security?" (November 1968); Oded Remba, "The Real State of Israel's Economy" (December 1968); and D. C. Watt, "Why There Is No Commercial Future for the Suez Canal" (January 1969); Watt's views are challenged by Peregrine Fellowes, "The

Suez Canal: Highway or Dead End?" (June 1971). Much relevant data has been assembled (but with little emphasis on underlying trends) by Eliyahu Kanovsky in his *Economic Impact of the Six-Day War* (New York, 1970). No major assessment of the economic repercussions of the Yom Kippur War has yet appeared.

INDEX